ABOUT ROB COUTEAU:

Positive reviews of Rob Couteau's books have appeared in the *Midwest Book Review*, *Publishers Weekly Select*, and Barney Rosset's *Evergreen Review*. In 1985 he won the North American Essay Award, a competition sponsored by the American Humanist Association. His work as a critic, interviewer, and social commentator has been featured in books such as *Gabriel Garcia Marquez's 'Love in the Time of Cholera'* by Thomas Fahy, *Conversations with Ray Bradbury* edited by Steven Aggelis, *Ghetto Images in Twentieth-Century American Literature* by Tyrone R. Simpson, and David Cohen's *Forgotten Millions*, a book about the homeless mentally ill. Over one-hundred selections of his poetry and prose have appeared in over forty-five periodicals. Couteau's interviews include conversations with Ray Bradbury, Pulitzer Prize-winning author Justin Kaplan, *Last Exit to Brooklyn* novelist Hubert Selby, Simon & Schuster editor Michael Korda, LSD discoverer Dr. Albert Hofmann, Picasso's model and muse Sylvette David, Nabokov biographer Robert Roper, music producer Danny Goldberg, poet and publisher Ed Foster, and historian Philip Willan, author of *Puppetmasters: The Political Use of Terrorism in Italy*.

ROB COUTEAU

Collected Couteau:

Essays and Interviews

Third, Revised Edition

DOMINANTSTAR

Dominantstar, New York.

The writing in this book is a work of fiction. Names, characters, places, and incidents either are products of the author's imagination or are used fictitiously. Any resemblance to actual events, locales, or persons, living or dead, is coincidental.

Third, revised edition. 1 2 3 4 5 6 7 8 9 10 01

Excerpts from this collection have previously appeared in a slightly altered form in the following publications: *Arete; Journal of Contemporary Psychotherapy; Lift; Nice; Paris Voice; Quantum; Rain Taxi Review of Books;* and *West Hills Review: A Walt Whitman Journal*.

This edition is dedicated to Yongzhen Zhang.

Cover: Photo of Rob Couteau in Paris, circa 1989.

Dominantstar LLC:
dominantstarpublications.com

Author's web site:
robcouteau.com

Paperback ISBN: 978-0-9966888-3-3
E-book ISBN: 978-0-9966888-9-5

CONTENTS

For Yongzhen Zhang

A Sort of Visitor in Life

At all times, perhaps, the central point in any nation ... is in its national literature, especially its archetypal poems.
– Walt Whitman, *Democratic Vistas*, 1871.

Reading Whitman always prompts the question: How could he have been an American? For he emerges as her most anomalous personification. Yet, with the exception of Tom Paine, he alone embodies all that is American in the ideal sense of the word. Without these two figures, everything proclaimed in the Declaration of Independence, the Constitution, and the Bill of Rights remains an abstraction, a mere potentiality.

I invoke Paine at the inception of an essay on Whitman not because of any direct influence of Paine on the poet but because of the link in spirit they share. That Whitman was more than superficially aware of Paine's significance is revealed in his speech, "In Memory of Thomas Paine," delivered in Philadelphia 140 years after Paine's birthday: "I dare not say how much of what our Union is owning and enjoying today ... is owing to Thomas Paine." The confessionalist Frank Harris attended the event in the role of a reporter. In *My Life and Loves*, he writes: "Nothing could be more depressing than the aspect of the hall that night: ill-lit and half-heated, with perhaps thirty people scattered about in a space that would have accommodated a thousand. Such was the reception America afforded to one of its greatest spirits." Like Paine, Whitman called American society to task. He demanded it awake and assume a posture that could truly be hailed as heroic.

While Paine was instrumental in the formation of the Republic, Whitman came of age after the last of the "Founding Fathers" had passed away. What remained of an idyllic, pastoral America was now rapidly fading into the shadow of a dreary machine age. (How fittingly "modern" that a revolution of machines–the Industrial Revolution– had usurped the infinitely more human Revolution that Paine had been instrumental in catalyzing!) Paine was the first to coin the term "The United States of America," was one of the first to write against slavery, and had a central role in formulating the ideas behind the Declaration. ("That he inspired the Declaration of Independence and is the godfather of the free American nation is either unknown or disregarded," writes Paine's sympathetic biographer, W. E. Woodward.) That he was an ordinary "commoner" rather than an aristocrat or a man of wealth had much to do with why the document doesn't bear his signature, as it had much to do with why he was ostracized by upper-class "democrats" throughout his life. Nevertheless, in his *Age of Reason* and *Rights of Man*, he continued to explore his vision of the elementary "rights of man," which he first articulated in his influential *Common Sense* publications.

In a strikingly similar fashion, Whitman took it upon himself to redefine and amplify what he felt to be at the core of the American soul. To do so, he grabs the torch directly from the hands of Paine. He stretches towards him unencumbered–without an obstacle–as the cultural void greatest spirits." Like Paine, Whitman called American society to task. He demanded it awake and assume a posture that could truly be hailed as heroic.

While Paine was instrumental in the formation of the Republic, Whitman came of age after the last of the

"Founding Fathers" had passed away. What remained of an idyllic, pastoral America was now rapidly fading into the shadow of a dreary machine age. (How fittingly "modern" that a revolution of machines–the Industrial Revolution–had usurped the infinitely more human Revolution that Paine had been instrumental in catalyzing!) Paine was the first to coin the term "The United States of America," was one of the first to write against slavery, and had a central role in formulating the ideas behind the Declaration. ("That he inspired the Declaration of Independence and is the godfather of the free American nation is either unknown or disregarded," writes Paine's sympathetic biographer, W. E. Woodward.) That he was an ordinary "commoner" rather than an aristocrat or a man of wealth had much to do with why the document doesn't bear his signature, as it had much to do with why he was ostracized by upper-class "democrats" throughout his life. Nevertheless, in his *Age of Reason* and *Rights of Man*, he continued to explore his vision of the elementary "rights of man," which he first articulated in his influential *Common Sense* publications.

In a strikingly similar fashion, Whitman took it upon himself to redefine and amplify what he felt to be at the core of the American soul. To do so, he grabs the torch directly from the hands of Paine. He stretches towards him unencumbered–without an obstacle–as the cultural void within which these two are left to wander is of staggering immensity.

Indeed, the genesis of a Whitman or a Paine is nearly inexplicable: enshrouded in mystery. With Paine we can at least point to a European birth and upbringing. But in the case of Whitman, there remains not a single clue–neither in his biography nor in the history of his country–that serves to anticipate the birth of *Leaves of Grass* or the man who engendered it. (One biographer considers it reminiscent of the biographical gap in the New Testament chronicle of Christ.) Yet the search for such "causes" is always futile. In Whitman's own words, "To elaborate is to no avail, learned and unlearned feel that it is so." If anything, such gaps reflect something symbolic. They point to all that recedes before such an analytical beacon. In the words of his devout disciple, Dr. Bucke, we must content ourselves with an intuitive term–*enlightenment*–and leave it at that.

"I shall use the words America and democracy as convertible terms," writes Whitman. He envisions democracy as the mundane counterpart of its metaphysical equivalent: the spiritually equalizing factor of the soul that, with its manifold potential, renders each a divine equal. "For after the rest is said," he writes, "it remains to bring forward and modify everything else with the idea of that Something a man is (last precious consolation of the drudging poor), standing apart from all else, divine in his own right, and a woman in hers, sole and untouchable by any canons of authority." Of the same notion, he chants, in poetic form:

> Is it you that thought the President greater than you?
> Or the rich better off than you? or the educated wiser
> than you?
> Because you are greasy or pimpled or were once drunk,
> or a thief,
> Or that you are diseas'd, or rheumatic, or a prostitute,
>
> Or from frivolity or impotence, or that you are no scholar
> and never saw your name in print,
> Do you give in that you are any less immortal?

Opposed to this special notion of democracy, Whitman posited *individuality*. He defines this as an American ideal that opposes the psychology of the aggregate: "The two are contradictory, but our task is to reconcile them." And he imagines a means of unifying such seeming opposites: "I say the mission of government, henceforth, in civilized lands, is ... to train communities through all their grades, beginning with individuals and ending there again, to rule themselves."

Reflecting his idea of democracy and individuality as opposites out of which a third element might emerge, he himself exemplifies such a synthesis. Thus, a century before Max Imboden envisioned "the State [as] a reflection of psychic reality," and "Democracy [as] ... the State form of citizens when all or the majority among them have reached a sufficient degree of individuation, so that they are clearly aware of their mutual relationship, and become able to create an authentic community," we have Whitman: an amalgam born of such seemingly antagonistic elements.

It's in this context that I view Whitman as an atypical American yet our most American American: atypical because so highly individuated; ideally American because this individuation, which cast Whitman in stark contrast to the society of his time, was the *sine qua non* of the democratic consciousness as defined by Whitman and, years later, by Imboden. Therefore, from Whitman's "I shall use the words America and democracy as convertible terms," we may conclude that, for him, the ideal American consciousness is synonymous with democratic consciousness, which is synonymous with individuated consciousness.

Thus, in Whitman's incarnation an essential aspect of the American ideal is realized. Contemplating this, we are jolted by unfamiliar, nearly incomprehensible imagery. We observe him lingering with a hulking yet tranquil poise;

with a piercing, sagelike gaze; with an aura detached yet erotic. In him is embodied a vast array of opposites. Most glaring is the polarity that energizes the *Leaves* from its core: the incarnation of the godhead in man. It finds expression in a Whitman photo that Dr. Bucke refers to as "the Christ-likeness." To be human and divine! It's not a typical American aspiration, nor is it an integral aspect of the so-called American Dream:

> Divine am I inside and out, and I make holy whatever I
> touch or am touch'd from,
> The scent of these arm-pits aroma finer than prayer, This
> head more than churches, bibles, and all the creeds.

Whitman points to what lies in veiled, cryptic form at the root of all Americanisms (or any *ism*, for that matter): the divine urge towards individuation; the kernel that lies at the source of the thought "Become what thou art," as proclaimed by the Greek poet Pindar.

Yet, when the divine instinct remains unrecognized, it is forced to resurface in cruder, collective, less conscious guises. Then the spiritual urge is turned upside down, the State becomes God, and the soul is lured by fanaticism, greed, lust, and power. Whether in its stultified, destructive manifestation or in its humanistic creative aspect, however, we discover–hidden beneath and beyond everything–the divine passion play of the spirit: draped in the language of symbol and revealing the patterns of the eternal.

It is at this precipice of consciousness that Whitman arrives. He gazes down at the unraveling carpet of the nineteenth century. His vision recedes to the primal eons and then refocuses at the threshold of the future. He's become so American that he passes beyond the meridian of the American ideal and begins traveling in retrograde. In his molting, he disregards not only everything American but anything even vaguely cultural. From this point onward, he uses the American idiom simply as a means of remaining intelligible. Sometimes he uses it symbolically; sometimes metaphorically. He uses it interchangeably, to mean far more or far less than his countrymen will ever suppose. All the while, his hand remains gripped to the mystic-poetic root. His being sprouts from it, like a massive appendage through which emerge the most arcane, esoteric revelations.

Out of this silent molting is dropped the *Leaves*. Reading it, many are struck by what might be termed a *sanctified immorality*. Whitman was a dignified sinner. Yet, to read his biography is to witness an extermination of the sin-concept by a fireball of self-confidence. Actually, it's *Self* confidence: an experience of a transpersonal Self that propels him to his destiny. In the ordinary man "sin" begets guilt, which, if properly integrated, will elevate the seeker to a new level of awareness. In Whitman, however, the sin concept is annihilated–he's several centuries beyond it. Guilt, too, is antiquated. In their stead is a gnostic intuition born of this Self awareness.

We have only to contemplate a song such as "A Woman Waits for Me"–that erotic testament of man's relationship to cosmos–to observe exactly where he has arrived. What other nineteenth-century American poet would compose a song to his Puritan brethren wherein the sexual encounter is revealed to be the highest act of patriotism? And a *sacred* patriotism, through which the soul of a people is distilled and revealed!

This, one of Whitman's most provocative works, has been criticized by some as betraying an emotional detachment that is, at times, unnerving. Yet emotion is unmistakably present, but it's directed beyond the singular human figure. Instead, it's interwoven with divine elements. Whitman intimately embraced the fecundating force incarnated in the human being, which, simultaneously, remains beyond the merely human.

Perhaps, Whitman is best defined as a self-proclaimed poet of health. In his hands, vices are transformed into virtues; boundaries between good and evil are blurred; and social restrictions and regulations are redefined by the individuals they are meant to serve:

> What blurt is this about virtue and about vice?
> Evil propels me and reform of evil propels me....I stand
>   indifferent,
> My gait is no fault-finder's or rejecter's gait,
> I moisten the roots of all that has grown.

In *Specimen Days*, he writes of being "in solitude with Nature" when "Nature was naked, and I was also." He asks if nakedness is somehow indecent and answers, "No, not inherently. It is your thought, your sophistication, your fear, your respectability that is indecent."

For Whitman, nothing outdoes the sanctity of the body. In his finest "prayer" to it, *I Sing the Body Electric*, he proclaims:

> O my Body! I dare not desert the likes of you in other
> men and women, nor the likes of the parts of you,
> I believe the likes of you are to stand or fall with the
> likes of the Soul, (and that they are the Soul)

He writes of "The curious sympathy one feels when feeling with the hand / The naked meat of the body," and he asks,

"And if the body were not the Soul, what is the Soul?" Of loafing, which assumes a colossal importance in his life, he writes, "Of all human beings, none equals your genuine, inbred, unvarying loafer. What was Adam, I should like to know, but a loafer?"

Like Adam, Whitman is too close to the source to bother hustling and bustling. What matter if, unlike Adam, he lived in an America bursting at the seams in the midst of a frenetic Industrial Revolution? No matter. He refuses to budge from the womb of Mother Nature. She nourishes him with such vitality that he sees no reason to abandon her. Instead, he digs himself in deeper. He converts his world to a womb cosmos simply by imagining it as such.

From this unique vantage point, he reveals images and aspects of the transformation process that are foreign even to his own understanding. "There is that in me–I do not know what it is–but I know / it is in me." "Pointing in silence to these songs, and then to the sand beneath, I perceive I have not really understood anything, not a / single object, and that no man ever can." It's like inquiring of the womb whether it comprehends its own creation. Eventually, he becomes womblike himself: a sort of microcosmic "womb within a womb." It's as if, for an entire lifetime, he's forced to simulate the conditions of the womb so as to make possible the proper incubation of the *Leaves*. The external world confronts him with its energetic, phallic aspect, and he becomes intrigued by its penetrations and provocations. Yet he continues to assume a passive, receptive attitude: one staggering in its stillness. "Urge and urge and urge, / Always the procreant urge of the world."

I see lurking throughout Whitman's life a desire to return to the Great Cosmic Mother and, therefore, to the mystery of death itself. It is regressive but also progressive–one senses a yearning to uncover the final veil. She is the source of the death musings that appear throughout his poetry. It is she who lures him to the promenades he was so fond of taking through Brooklyn's Greenwood Cemetery. The unavoidable prospect of returning to her haunches both fascinates and horrifies him. In "Song of Myself," he taunts: "And as to you Death, and you bitter hug of mortality, it is idle to try to alarm me." Elsewhere he writes: "Creeping thence steadily up to my ears and laving me softly all over, / Death, death, death, death, death."

How apropos that, at age sixty-five–before he owned the simple, unpretentious house he was to die in–he built, with funds donated for the purpose of constructing a summer home, a mausoleum: one massive and archaic in appearance, and seemingly indestructible. (It was fashioned after a drawing left by his predecessor, William Blake.) In his informative Whitman biography, Justin Kaplan writes, "Some of the blocks weighed eight or ten tons; the roof was a foot and a half thick." This was the "life" he thought worthy of preparing for: at rest in a monumental abode, wherein he and his family members would partake of the voluptuous stillness of eternity. How fitting and true are the words of the naturalist John Burroughs, who said of Whitman: "He seems always to have been a sort of visitor in life."

His songs are so ripe with prophetic utterance that we are astonished to consider they were penned in any age other than our own. And many appear to be encoded in a language from some future epoch. While we often speak of artists "standing the test of time," with Whitman we confront a man who *is* one with the river of time. His songs radiate from him, like eddies resplendent with a luster of eternality.

Published in *West Hills Review,* 1985 (Huntington Station, NY).

Defining the Sacred: Author Hubert Selby on Spirituality, the Creative Will, and Love

Couteau: You've just returned from Europe where you gave a series of readings in Germany and attended the Paris premiere of the documentary, *A Couple of Things about Hubert Selby.* Would you care to relate some of the highlights of your recent trip?

Selby: Oh, gee, I don't know if there were any highlights, to tell you the truth. It was all very exciting. I enjoyed all of it. And after the people down in the breakfast room at the hotel saw me on television, I got extra croissants in the morning. So, that was kind of nice. Well, the people were all so wonderful; the reception was so enthusiastic, that I can't think of anything that stands out more than anything else. Other than some of the scenery. Berlin was incredible; there are forests and lakes all over that city. It was just amazing.

Couteau: In that film, you were asked about your belief in God, and you said it all depends on one's definition of God: that you didn't believe in most of the conventional definitions, the way that most people define God. Now, my question is, do you have any spiritual beliefs? I'm not going to ask, "Do you believe in God"; that's not really how I would phrase it, perhaps. But do you have any specific spiritual beliefs and, if so, what is your definition of the sacred?

Selby: Well, I don't know if I can define it. I certainly do attempt to live according to spiritual principles. That's al-

ways the foundation of each and every day. But to define ...
I don't think you can. I think anything that I can define is
not it. It has to be beyond my ability to define or
understand. But I have experienced some things in my life
that just force me to believe in some sort of power. A
creative ... power, source ... however you want to phrase it.
I certainly have experienced that presence. And I have
experienced the, what I consider the basic ... Oh, so hard to
use words to describe an ultradimensional thing. But what
we would call love and concern.

Couteau: Do you feel that this thing that is so difficult to
give a name to–as Lao Tsu says, "The Tao that can be
named is not the true Tao" ...

Selby: [laughs] That's right, "is not the Tao," that's right!
Couteau: This thing that is so hard to define, is it
something that just exists on a human level or on a profane
level, or is it something that, for lack of a better word, we
could call extramundane or spiritual? Do you believe in
anything like that?

Selby: Oh, yeah, absolutely. I believe in something that is
beyond this body. And beyond this physical world.
Absolutely.

Couteau: That's always been the sense that I get from
your writing. When he was close to death, Henry Miller
said he did not believe in God in the first-person singular,
not as an "I," but that he did believe in creation, which is
very close, very similar to what you just said.

Selby: Yeah, I would say "it" rather than "I." [laughs]

Couteau: I noticed in a previous print interview that you
said you felt you were–I'm paraphrasing now–merely an
"agent" of the creative. Where, then, does it come from?

And how is the artist's spiritual role different from the role that ordinary people play?

Selby: Well, what do you mean where does "it"? What is "it"? Do you mean where does this ultimate creative force come from?

Couteau: I think I'm asking you, in the role of a writer–because you were talking about being a writer–and then, you know, when you write, as I think we all feel when we're suddenly inspired, there's something coming from beyond us.

Selby: Oh, right. Well, beyond? I wouldn't say beyond. I would say absolutely within. But I couldn't limit the depth of "within." Because once you start getting within, you are in such a boundless, infinite universe. But it's important for me to say within, because I don't think there's anything outside of me.

Couteau: Are you part of that big "it" with a capital *I*, then?

Selby: I think we all are, yes. Absolutely. See, which is interesting, because, obviously, every second of every day, people are being born, people are dying, which means whatever this "it" is, *changes*. It's in constant change, constant flux. Yet, I want to keep it still. [laughs] And I think that's the source of so many of my problems, and I guess you could say the world's problems, is that we're trying to control it, instead of just surrendering to it.

Couteau: You've said, "Sometimes we have the absolute certainty that there's something inside us that's so hideous and monstrous that, if we ever search it out, we won't be able to stand looking at it. But it's when we're willing to come face-to-face with that demon that we face the angel." Do you believe in angels?

Selby: I'm just using, you know, the vernacular here–demons, angels–but, yeah, I do believe ... [pauses] See, again, *angels* is a tough word, because it is so involved with organized religion and everything else. But let me just say this: I do know, absolutely, from my experience, there are some kind of spiritual entities–force, power, intelligence–that guide me through each and every day, as long as I'm willing to accept, recognize, and surrender to their guidance. It's always there, but there are times when I insist upon having my way.

Couteau: That's wonderful that you say that. I think this gets close to what I was trying to understand, which is that you do feel there are extrahuman powers or forces that move through us. Is that correct?

Selby: Yeah. But I suppose you could get right down to it and say, well, maybe they're not even extrahuman, maybe they're ultrahuman; who knows? But there are definitely things that aren't necessarily walking around [laughs] in a body like mine. And I believe they're sort of everywhere. I mean, I can't ... You know, where can you look where you're not looking in the direction of God so to speak? Where do I go where I'm not surrounded by air, and all these little molecules and atoms, and all that kind of stuff that's there? It's just there.

Couteau: That may work as a good segue into a question I was going to ask further down the line. Because it makes me think of "Psalm 16," what you just said. You know, your piece "Psalm 16"?

Selby: Oh ... oh, *mine*. Yeah, okay; I was thinking of David's [laughs]–I couldn't remember 16!

Couteau: [laughs] Okay! My question was: Are good and evil two sides of the same face of God? I'm remembering your stunning piece, "Psalm 16," in which you excoriate God and all that occurs "in your name, in your fucking myriad of names." Such a beautiful line! And on the other hand, you sing, at the end of that psalm: "I said to the almond tree, 'Speak to me of God.' And the almond tree blossomed."

Selby: Precisely. One of the things I like about ... *Whew*, I get chills thinking about it! One of the things I like about that psalm is that it appears that the narrator doesn't know what he's doing [laughs] or what he's saying. He doesn't realize he's defeating his own argument so to speak. That's one of the things I like about it.

See, the thing is, about the face of God ... again, that really personalizes it, doesn't it, when we say, "the face of God"? And then that gets us back to that Henry Miller thing and so forth. So, I don't think they're two different faces of God. I think "good and evil" is simply my perception of something at the moment.

Couteau: Do you believe in evil as an independent, autonomous force that acts within us or against us? Or is evil, as the Church has sometimes defined it, merely the "absence of good?"

Selby: I don't seem to be capable of believing in evil as some separate, distinct power within itself. I guess I'm just not a Southern Baptist or a Fundamentalist [laughs]. I just don't seem to be capable of believing in it, somehow. I can't conceive, from my experience, how this force of evil can exist without the force of love being right there.

Couteau: When I read through your books, there is, omnipresent, the term and image and notion of the *demon*.

Selby: That's right.

Couteau: And in this world of duality, naturally, the question would be: Well, what's the counterpoint of the demon? Which is why I asked about the angels.

Selby: Well, actually, the counterpoint is love. As I understand it, there are only two emotions a human being can experience: love or fear. And when you're in a state of love, you can't think of trying to *get* anything. You're incapable of thinking that way. You just seem to experience the perfection of creation and want to do what you can to make everyone comfortable; you just give away everything you have. When I talk about giving away, I'm not talking about my clothes or my house–from within me. You know, try to comfort people.

If I'm coming from anyplace else, I'm coming from fear. And fear takes many, many, many forms to be effective. *All kinds* of forms. So, if I'm facing the demon of fear, love is always available. But what I have to do is to be willing to *surrender* to it. Surrender my ideas: of what is right, what is wrong, and all those dreadful judgments that keep us in turmoil and ignorance and misery.

Couteau: Are the demons merely what Jung would call "autonomous complexes"? Are they things that are just below consciousness, that are pulling us in the wrong direction, and that have been formed by past experiences?

Selby: I really couldn't say. I don't know if it's formed by past experience. I mean, because then, if you say past experiences, now we're getting into reincarnation …

Couteau: Well, I actually meant in this lifetime.

Selby: Well, no, I don't think so. It seems to be something else. I mean, then how would you explain Mozart?

Couteau: I think Mozart, like you, is an example of someone who has the gods moving through him, and his religion was creation.

Selby: Yeah, and at three years old he's writing music! [laughs] I mean … [laughs] you know? So, I don't know.

How about the accident of birth? Maybe you're *born* with an obsession or that aspect of obsession that just has to be generated, somehow, through life. I just don't know.

Couteau: So you do feel it's possible that, as the word *destiny* implies–"that which follows from before"–you do believe we may be born into this world not coming in with a blank slate, so to speak?

Selby: Right. I do believe that. I don't believe in a blank slate in any way. I mean, that's what we seem to be taught, at least in the Western world: we're born with a blank slate, and we have to learn how to get and get. Otherwise, we're *fucked*. [laughs] That seems to be the message, you know! Certainly, in this country.

But no one ever seems to train us in methods of finding out that we already have within us all the things that are valuable: all the treasures. But it's only in the process of giving them away, to somebody else, that we become aware of having them.

And I don't know; I just don't know about where these things, where do my obsessions come from? My earliest memory as a little kid: I have these obsessions. I have no idea. I'm grateful I found out how I can become increasingly free of them. But I don't know. And I don't know anything really about karma, reincarnation. So, I can't explain the origin.

Couteau: Do you believe that love is something that existed before human beings? Or the possibility for it existed before we came down the block?

Selby: Well, yeah, I think so, but I don't know that I could really define it. I can't ... again, it's like trying to define what this creative force is. It's beyond my ability to really define. If I can define it, then it's not it. We're right back to that thing again.

Couteau: We're back to Lao Tsu.

Selby: Yeah, right back there again. So, I don't know. But I do believe that what we call love is always available to us. And of course, I'm not just talking about passion. I'm talking about love where you just can't conceive that your life isn't perfect: that you can't conceive of *wanting* anything.

Couteau: Do you mean love that could exist without another person?

Selby: Yes, oh, yes. In one sense: in an experiential sense. But if love is what I've experienced, I can't separate it from other people. I can't separate creation, and I can't separate whatever this creative thing is from *its creation*. I don't believe that can be done. So, as I said before, we're all part of this creative force. So, where else am I going to be directing my love? Now, I can sit alone and experience this thing and be overwhelmed with such ecstasy that I can't say anything but "thank you." But ultimately, I direct it towards people. Hopefully.

Couteau: Is it directed into your work?

Selby: Well, yeah. But of course, then again, we get down to a definition ... It may be hard to find the love in my work sometimes! [laughs] We'll put it that way! According to the way people define love.

Couteau: I think I meant: is the act of you sitting down, with all your physical pain, and all the things you've been through, and all the difficulties that every writer encounters in writing a book–isn't it really motivated by love?

Selby: Yeah. And that love is beyond what we call love. That's something ... it's probably beyond what any writer calls love, too! [laughs]

Couteau: It's not romantic love we're talking about; we're talking about rapture.

Selby: Yeah, we're talking about rapture; we're talking about creation. We're also talking about extraordinary pain.

Couteau: Which brings us back to what we were talking about before: what I called, for lack of a better metaphor, the two sides of the face of the absolute. There was a German philosopher who wrote about comparative religion; his name was Rudolf Otto. He wrote a book called *The Idea of the Holy*. He invented two terms. He said the encounter with the absolute is either a *mysterium fascinans* or a *mysterium tremendum*. It can be bliss or it can be terror. Or it can be both.

As a spiritual man, is it difficult to reconcile the pain that you were just speaking of: that it's part of this creation, too? That there are demons; that that's all part of the same portrait?

Selby: Oh, yeah, it's difficult. At least for me. Sometimes I sit here, and the phone rings, and I cry. "I ... I can't talk!" I'm just totally incapable of it. But I've come to believe, from my experience, that whenever I feel like I'm locked in hell, I am at the gates of heaven. And my perception of my experience can change in the wink of an eye. Just all of a sudden. *Boom.*

Couteau: You're at the gates of heaven, because that can be the next step? Or ... ?

Selby: Let me put it this way. I think we're always striving for this perfection of our own being: to *realize* our own perfection. To realize and to be consciously at one with this thing that created us that we always have within us.

I mean, we always have it in its entirety. It's my belief that says, "I don't." And it seems to me that, periodically, the closer I get to the conscious awareness of my oneness with this creative power, the more insane the human ego becomes. And I'm defining "ego" as the lie of separation. The lie that says I'm separate from this thing that I can never be separate from. I'm separate from me; I'm separate from you. It starts to feel really threatened, and it just becomes outrageously vicious. At its best, [laughs] it's vicious. And so, I can just feel so twisted and turned that I can't move. I just don't know what the hell is going on.

But my experience has proven to me that when I'm feeling that way, it's because I'm really knocking at the gates of heaven. You know, to use a phrase. And if I can just find some way of letting go of my fear, which usually means surrendering right into the middle of the fear–in other words, just sitting and saying: Okay, you fucking dragons, you demons, here I am: eat me up alive, you fucking punk– then I become aware of being at the gates of heaven. But boy, it's not easy. [laughs]

Couteau: I recently reread *Last Exit to Brooklyn* while simultaneously reading your last book, *The Willow Tree*. Most critics remember your first book for its portrayal of absolute brutality and cruelty–and maybe we can say, in this context, separation, right?

Selby: Mm-hmm.

Couteau: While the last book is, in part, highlighted by the attempt of various characters to show empathy, passion, and love. Yet, a careful reading reveals that there are episodes, incidents, and moments in *Last Exit* in which empathy occurs, and it's portrayed in a beautiful and touching manner.

Selby: I think so, you know? [laughs] I'm glad to hear that you do!

Couteau: I'm also thinking of the story, "And Baby Makes Three," which, at least in part, is about "having a ball" as one character says. More specifically, in "The Queen is Dead," there are moving passages that portray Georgette's love for Vinnie.

I was surprised to discover three principal symbols that make their appearance in this chapter: the swan, the lake, and the willows. These symbols of rapture and bliss also appear years later, in your last book, *The Willow Tree*: specifically, the part where Moishe takes Bobby to Prospect Park, and Bobby experiences what may be his first day of pure rapture and bliss. Are things such as happiness, bliss, ecstasy, and rapture among the most difficult themes or portrayals to handle successfully as a writer?

Selby: I think so. Because for one thing, like you said, this is a world of duality, so we need something to compare it with. So I have to set the situation up where we can experience the difference between whatever we are having–everyday life–and this experience of bliss.

You said Bobby's first experience of bliss was being under the willow tree with Moishe. But remember, later on, when Bobby tries to remember some time in his life that made a difference? He remembers when he was a little kid, and they opened up the hydrant on a summer day. And he had that moment then. You see what I mean? It's a very relative thing. But he had a brief time there, where: oh, life was just *enchantment*. "Even the old cranky folks" or "the old sour pusses, were okay." [Quoting from memory, from the passage.]

Couteau: If I recall correctly, he remembers that when he's with Moishe in the park, right?

Selby: Mm-hmm. I think so.

Couteau: Why is it so much more difficult to portray happiness–and to make the critics happy about how you portray it?

Selby: I don't know how to make the critics happy! [laughs] I mean, this book, *The Willow Tree*: I can't even get criticism in this country; that's been totally ignored.

Couteau: I remember reading something that Norman Mailer once said: that people get uncomfortable when you talk about being in love. People get uncomfortable when they hear a description of pure happiness, and they tend to look at it as being silly. Maybe it's just a general human reaction.

Selby: Quite often, if you're talking about being in love, you probably sound very silly, because, for one thing, you're totally self-centered at that time, aren't you? When we're talking about romantic love and so on. That must be what he's referring to.

Now, to talk about the subject of love in some undefined sense, that can be *fascinating*. But we don't get into that. We're talking about a very subjective, first-person sort of thing. And yeah, [laughs] that can be a bore! Because of the way we talk about it. But if we can present a *life*, with the tragedies and horrors of life, then see the absence of these horrors ...

You see, I discovered something, many years ago. I spent so many years trying to get happy that I finally realized that I can't get happy: that happiness is a natural state of being. When I stop doing the things that make me unhappy, I will experience the happiness that is a natural state of being.

See, I don't think we were created with some *pain*, and *misery*, and whatever. I think we were created by whatever this thing is–when it *extended* itself–and here we are. But I pile on so many misconceptions that I end up uncomfortable in my own skin.

Couteau: That's similar to the other definition I mentioned before if we turn it around and speak of good as "the absence of evil."

Selby: In a very real sense, yes. But the problem with that definition is the way that it's phrased–"good is the absence of evil"–as if it's not something absolute within itself. Now, I don't use the words "good" or "bad," I don't ...

Couteau: As if what's not something absolute in itself?

Selby: Well, what we're calling goodness, love, you see? But of course, in our experience, in the human condition, we do need both; it is a world of duality. So, I don't know from up without down, or left without right.

Couteau: Well, since we're in this metaphysical dilemma right now ...

Selby: [laughs] And have been for many moons, I guess!

Couteau: Right! This might be a good moment to ask: what's our purpose, then? I mean, in the really big sense of the question. And what's your purpose as a writer? When you wake up in the morning, and you're thinking about the book you're working on, what's the ultimate goal there?

Selby: When I'm thinking about the book I'm working on, the ultimate goal is always, of course, just simply to write the best book I can write and to understand the book that's been given to me to write. So that I can create it appropriately.

Now, I don't know about the meaning of life. You know, that's [laughs] ... There is no definition of it; it can only be *experienced*. But I do believe–and I think Moishe says this– that we all need a *meaning* to our life. I have to have a meaning in my life. If I roam around without some meaning in my life, I'm in deep and serious trouble. I can't, I just can't exist.

Couteau: The French have that wonderful expression, *raison d'être*: reason to be. If you had to define your *raison d'être*, what would you say, in a sentence?

Selby: To be as kind, gentle, loving as possible.

Couteau: What's wonderful about the things you're saying is that you have this very well articulated metaphysic–because it's coming from experience–but you bring it down-to-earth and continually return to those basic ... I could say moral qualities, right? Kindness, love, forgiveness. As a writer or as a person, would you define yourself, in part, as a moralist? Or is that just too small a word?

Selby: You know, I never thought of it in those terms. But I guess I'd have to, to some degree, because I am concerned with what the moral dynamic might be of any story that's given to me to write. Not only the psychodynamic but also what the moral dynamic is, is important. I mean, the first time somebody asked me to describe *Last Exit*, I heard myself say: "The horrors of a loveless world." And I think that's true, the more I ... And that's many moons ago that I was asked that question. I hadn't thought about it ahead of time, but that's what came out of my mouth.

And I can't find any reason to change my mind about that statement.

Couteau: I noticed in *The Willow Tree* that there are many times when the phrase "the demon" makes its appearance. And of course, there's your wonderful book by that same title. While rereading *Last Exit,* I noticed the first appearance in your writing of this word, the *demon*. It's when Georgette spontaneously decides to read Edgar Allan Poe's poem, "The Raven." She recites: "And his eyes have all the seeming of a demon's that is dreaming."

Now, when I met you in Paris, I was surprised to see that you were always smiling and laughing, and that your eyes did not have the seeming of a demon!

Selby: [laughs] Well, thank you!

Couteau: When I read that line, I thought: perhaps Selby is the demon that is dreaming, and what he dreams up is this collection of some of the best prose in American literature. Or one could say that the demon is another force that you've been selected to be the *agent* for–to use your term from before. If you are the agent, what is the price you pay for carrying the demon within you and for giving it a voice?

Selby: *Oh*, boy. The price! *Whew*. You know, first of all, you can't say with absolute certainty. However, I can say [laughs] that my life, to a great extent, has been a horror story. Whew.

In a way, I don't pay a price, but I'm given something. I have these experiences in my life. I've had a lot of problems. Certainly, a lot of physical problems as well as emotional problems and everything else. Now, when I finally accept the fact that I'm a writer and go through the *arduous* task [laughs] of developing that ability ...

See, you must remember that I have no natural talents or abilities in any area of life. I'm not a natural writer or a natural reader; I'm not an exceptional mechanic; I'm not an exceptional athlete; I'm not a draftsman at all; I can't draw or ... Absolutely no natural talent. But I had an obsession to do something with my life before I died. And I just sat in front of that typewriter every day, for six years, until I learned how to write. Now, I can't say that the ability *wasn't* there, obviously. I guess it was there, and I just had to fight like hell to activate it, to animate it, to nurture it, to love it. So, I don't know about that. I just know that it was a lot, a lot of work.

Now, because I have this life of suffering, with demons and all other forms of misery, now at least I can do something with it. So it becomes for me ... I have to assume it becomes cathartic, in a sense. But at the same time, I have a certain framework.

Something else that kept me in conflict and created great pain is that, philosophically and consciously, ethically, morally, whatever, I'm a very pacifistic person. I don't believe in violence. Yet my life has been so violent that I'm constantly–at least, in the past–violating my own code of ethics and morality. And that is just destroying me. So, although I'm not consciously aware of this (I'm just looking back; I'm not aware of it at the time), I can constantly experience the difference between heaven and hell, so to speak. And the terrible pain of these conflicts and the *angst* of not doing the loving things that I always wanted to do. And doing all the mean-spirited things that I knew no human being should ever do.

So in the end result, I'm not focusing on any of these things; I'm focusing on writing the best story I can write. Which means I'm doing everything I can to give the artist within me as much power as possible. Then, somehow, on this piece of paper emerges the result of that conflict, in such a way that the reader can experience and see what it's really like to live this life. Instead of sitting comfortably somewhere and saying, "Oh, those people, they should all be *shot*."

Couteau: With your creative obsession with demonology; with God; with man's suffering and the possibility of redemption, catharsis, or even transcendence, which you've lately explored in *The Willow Tree*, aren't you in fact a religious writer?

Selby: Again, it depends on how we define the word *religious*. Certainly not in the organized sense, but in some very, very broad spiritual sense I guess I'd have to agree with you. Again, this wasn't my conscious effort in writing. But it seems to me I am. And I should amend my previous statement by saying, in *The Willow Tree*, it *was* a conscious effort to write a spiritual book.

Couteau: Could you elaborate on that?

Selby: Well, as simply as possible, I had spent many years writing about the darkness. And I wrote about the darkness from many different points of view, as I felt like it. And now I wanted ... See, I'm always presenting myself with problems to solve as a writer. So, the problem I presented myself with was: not only to write about the darkness but to write about the *light*. And how you get from the darkness to the light. So, I would think that that's kind of defining a spiritual book.

Couteau: Coming from Brooklyn myself, I'm always amazed at how much you've captured of that nearly impossible to describe place. If you hadn't been raised in Bay Ridge but, instead, had hailed from a small town with white picket fences, and year-round sunshine, and strangers who greeted everyone on Main Street by saying "Good morning" ... In other words, if the peculiar spirit of those dark Brooklyn streets had not infused itself into your soul, what do you think would have been the result? I mean, in terms of your writing.

Selby: Maybe I never would have written. That's quite possible, you know? Because one of the things that fascinates me is the music of speech. How many places are there in the world where you have the music of speech? Certainly not in most of this country. So, I just don't know. And if I had the same kind of personality that I have, living in a small town, I don't know if I would have survived long enough to try to write.

Couteau: One of the strange things about a lot of those parts of Brooklyn is that they don't seem to change, decade after decade.

Selby: Oh, that's right. Yeah, Bay Ridge, I think, is the same for the last eighty years. With a few physical exceptions.

Couteau: In many ways it's a wonderful place, but, in other ways, it's a very violent place. For some reason, there are a lot of violent people that come out of those streets.

Selby: Mm-hmm.

Couteau: And people who don't really have a sense of what you were calling *catharsis*.

Selby: But isn't it funny that all these mass murderers, and kids, and grown-ups who go around whacking people don't come from ...

Couteau: They come from the little towns with the white picket fences!

Selby: That's right! [laughs] Yeah, they don't come from Brooklyn. So, I might have been one of those! Given the nature of my personality. Who the heck knows? You know? I don't know, man; I don't know. But I know that I love the city; I love the *sound* of the city.

Couteau: I guess the other side of my question really was: how much of *Last Exit* and some of the things that followed, even up through and including *The Willow Tree*, how much of that is really a portrait of such streets? All your books are universal, but if someone like me has actually come from a place like that we're especially impressed, because it's a universal tale but it also mirrors and captures the uniqueness of that place. Is that something you've thought about through your life?

Selby: Well, not in the physical sense of portraying Brooklyn in any way. But in a very real sense, I have thought about it. Because what I attempt to do is put the reader through an emotional experience. So, you don't find much physical description in my work. I don't describe the streets too much or anything else. But I try to get as deeply inside the people who live on those streets as possible. I think that's what you're experiencing: what it's like to live on those streets. You're getting each individual's reaction to their life on those streets. Maybe that's what it is. I certainly can't really say.

Couteau: I know you feel a spiritual or literary kinship with Céline.

Selby: Yeah.

Couteau: There's another great writer who also emerged from Brooklyn who had a great kinship with Céline: that is, Henry Miller. Did Miller in any way influence you as a writer?

Selby: No ... I don't know how much of Miller I ever read before I started writing.

Couteau: There probably wasn't much available at that time.

Selby: No, there wasn't. Because I started writing in the mid '50s. So, no, I don't think ... even if I had read it, I don't think Miller would have influenced me in any way, because we seem to approach things so differently.

Couteau: How so?

Selby: Well, in a lot of ... Well, I don't know about "a lot"; I haven't read that much ...

Couteau: Oh, really? I thought he might've been someone you've read a lot, because I saw somewhere that you had his books on your bookshelf.

Selby: Yeah, I do have a couple of his books here. But

you know, some of his books ... See, I always have a very definite story line. I'm like an old-fashioned writer: a beginning, middle, and end, kind of thing. And quite often he doesn't. He just kind of wanders around in the streets of Paris, so to speak. And then he wanders around in his mind, you know? Just kind of strolling, straying. Which is cool; I'm not making a negative critique of this. But I think we approach things quite differently sometimes. Although that one book, I forget which *Tropic* it is, the one that takes place in Brooklyn when he's at Western Union: that had a pretty direct storyline, and was kind of linear, and there were some parts that had me laughing out loud. The thing with his first babysitter and all that kind of stuff, man, you know? [laughs]

Couteau: Do you like his writing?

Selby: Yeah. And the same thing with Céline; I don't think I've ever been influenced by Céline. But looking back on it, it just seems like–at least on the surface–it looks like I have more to do with him than anybody else. You know, in that raging, maniacal kind of sense.

Couteau: By the way, did you know that ... I don't think it's in print anywhere, but, apparently, Céline did use mescaline.

Selby: Oh, really?

Couteau: I was speaking with a biographer who had some contact with Allen Ginsberg, who had met Céline, and according to Ginsberg, Céline had used mescaline. I've always wondered about the influence of mescaline on Céline's books, because there are passages in his work that are quite hallucinatory.

Selby: So in other words, he used it on a regular basis for a while? Not just as an experimental thing?

Couteau: I don't know. I think there's very little known about it. I've read most of the biographies that are available on him, and I've never seen it in print. But I know that he used it at least once, and that he had access to it as a doctor.

Selby: That's true, too.

Couteau: Have you ever used hallucinogens?

Selby: No. Well, I smoked grass, which is basically a hallucinogenic. But no, I never wanted to go near them.

Couteau: Did using drugs have any kind of positive influence on your writing? Or to put it in another way, were you able to take anything out of that experience and portray it or use it as material?

Selby: Well, yeah, *Requiem for a Dream*, obviously.

Couteau: What about how it might have affected you as a stylist? Or your use of language?

Selby: Gee, I don't think so. Because I didn't get involved with drugs until after *Last Exit* was published. And I think that the language, and style, and so forth, were pretty well established there.

Couteau: Carl Jung used to say that it took as much as twenty years for the collective consciousness to catch up with the contents of his books. How much time will pass before the public is able to understand books like *The Room* and *Requiem for a Dream*?

Selby: Well, now that's a good question; that's a very good question. The public doesn't seem to have such a problem with my books. It's the *academics* that do! [laughs]

Couteau: And the critics? Is that what you mean when you say academics?

Selby: Well, some critics have been very kind, very wonderful.

Couteau: You received some great reviews for those books.

Selby: Yeah! Oh! Oh, *The Room*? Got some ... Josephine Hendin and Dotson Rader! I mean, wow, I got incredible reviews. But nobody seems to know it exists. So, it's not so much the public. I find that when the public gets around to reading it, from the feedback I get from them, they seem to relate to the book and enjoy it and so forth. But I've been kind of ostracized, I think, by the academic community. As a matter-of-fact, after *Last Exit* was published, I was told by someone that there really was a conspiracy against the book, in that the large bookstores in New York would not display the book. They would sell it, but they wouldn't display it.

Couteau: *Last Exit* was banned in the U.K. but not in the States. Why was *Last Exit* allowed to be published in the United States in 1964, while *Tropic of Cancer*, which was a much less obscene book–by the classical definition–was banned until just a few years before that?*

Selby: I think because–now, I don't know–but what popped in mind is the fact that it *had been* banned for many years. His work had been banned here for many years. You could only smuggle it in and all that sort of stuff. So it had a different resistance and a different procedure to go through.

Couteau: It had an already established weight, a history that it had to deal with.

Selby: Right. Yeah. And of course, Barney Rosset took care of business and made it possible for a lot of things to happen.

Couteau: You were just talking about the fact that there was a conspiracy to create obstacles for *Last Exit*. Did the FBI ever open a file on you, and, if so, have you ever seen it or requested it?

Selby: Somebody once told me that they have a file on me, but I ...

Couteau: Never seen it?

Selby: No.

Couteau: Not curious?

Selby: No ... well, I suppose ... I don't even think about it. I mean, what the hell could ...

Couteau: Might be good for some laughs, no?

Selby: Yeah! [laughs] No, I think it would piss me off to think of all the time and money they're wasting–getting a file on *me*, for Christ's sake! Maybe we should do something more important with all this stuff!

Couteau: It pisses me off that people like Frank Sinatra get the Presidential Medal of Freedom, or whatever it's called ...

Selby: [laughs] Yeah!

Couteau: And not people like you!

Selby: [laughs]

Couteau: I mean, that really pisses me off!

Selby: You know, fuck the medal–I could use some money! [laughs]

Couteau: *Dough-ray-me*, right?

Selby: Yeah! And don't forget, sixteen years ago, I was on welfare for Christ's sake, with my son. We were on welfare for a year.

Couteau: Well, this is coming off the top of my head, but do you have anything to say about how America treats its artists? Or maybe not just America but governments in the world, in general? I mean, you must still have some bitterness about that, no?

Selby: No, not bitterness, I just ... I get sad sometimes. I was certainly sad at the time when, you know, you have to scrounge for money to support your family. And I never could really earn a living because of my physical condition, lack of education, and so forth. But you know, governments ... the only government I really know is this government. We don't have a cultural affairs department or anything like they have in some of the European countries. Now, whether that's any better or not, I don't know! I'm sure there are plenty of artists who really oppose all that bureaucracy dealing with the arts. But it would be nice if, somehow, you could get some *money*. You know, I've applied for the NEA a couple of times, and the Guggenheims, and things like that. And I've always been turned down by everybody. According to them, there are at least 2,000 writers in this country that are better than I am. Which could very well be true. And I would love to read them ...

Couteau: But the question is: where the hell are they? [laughs]

Selby: Yeah, where are they? [laughs] You know what I mean? [laughs] Where the hell are they? It's true.

Couteau: Henry Miller was also turned down for a Guggenheim.

Selby: Well, I can understand that–because he was a *dirty writer!* [laughs] You know, in those days? To write the way he was writing? You know.

Couteau: When Picasso was living in Paris, he was approached by a group of artists, and they asked him to sign a petition demanding that the government give more money to artists. And he refused to sign it. He said, of course I'm not going to sign that petition; the state, the government, is the *enemy*.

Selby: Mm-hmm. Well, but we must remember that he was a Communist, so his attitude was a little different. But that's why I say that I'm not sure if it's beneficial to have an official government bureau. And who's going to head it? Jessie Helms? [laughs uproariously] Dan Quayle, that's who! [laughs]

Couteau: Right! Talking about Murphy Brown!*

Selby: [laughs]

Couteau: If Murphy Brown gives him a hard time, what about Hubert Selby?

Selby: Oh, my goodness! [laughs] Yeah. So, I don't know about governments as far as individual artists are concerned. I suspect it wouldn't be worth it to have them poking around. I think it would be nice if governments could be a little more helpful with, say, orchestras, ballet companies, and so forth, which can't sustain themselves. Maybe they could get a tax break on tickets or something. There might be some way of doing it where they could keep them out of it. But the individual artists … I think we just have to go our own way.

Couteau: I agree with you.

Selby: Yeah?

Couteau: Yeah. I think in a way, the great irony or paradox about America is that it makes it so hard for the sensitive person, the artist, the impressionable person, the person whose *raison d'être* is to incarnate the creative will rather than to just make money, and yet that extreme difficulty that the culture poses for us has created some of the best artists in the last hundred years.

Selby: Correct.

Couteau: You would agree with that?

Selby: Oh, yeah. I mean, how is a pearl manufactured?

Couteau: Beautiful answer.

Selby: Right? Yeah, that seems to be a necessary part. Because the artist by definition is *outside* the mainstream of society. Wasn't it Yeats who said that the artist is the antenna of the race?* It's so true. It seems to me that what the artist sees is the simple and obvious that is invisible to everybody else. And it's always there; it's all around us. The artist magnifies what's invisible to other people so that they're capable of at least realizing there's something here.

Couteau: What is the artist's relationship to the childhood experience? Were you, for example, the classic "artist as a child": the sensitive, impressionable person?

Selby: Oh, God, yeah! Oh, Jesus! [laughs] And not only that–my name is *Hubert*, and I'm born and raised in *Brooklyn*! Everybody's Mikey, Vinnie, Tony–it was like being a Jew in an Irish neighborhood! [laughs] I mean, everybody's poking fun at me. And I could never, never deal with it. I could never deal with it. Oh, God almighty. And of course, I don't know that, inside, I'm different from anybody else. And everybody else seems to be taking care of business. And I'm in this constant turmoil. I see a cat going through a garbage can getting something to eat–I fall apart; I'm crying, I'm dying! I can't stand to look at it, you know? Oh, man. You know, bringing home crippled birds. You know, that kind of thing.

Couteau: Was there an adult who was any kind of a role model; or was there a singular defining experience in your childhood that marked you to be an artist, later on, do you think?

Selby: No, I think it's just something there. Again, it's that accident of birth that I don't understand. I think it can get nurtured. You see, you don't decide to be an artist; you accept the fact that you are. But you don't decide to be one.

Now, who the hell could be that *dumb*? Can you imagine deciding to live this kind of life? Oh, good Lord! [laughs]

Couteau: I don't know if you've ever seen Mircea Eliade's work on shamanism, but he says that when the old shaman, or when the tribe, decides to select the young boy who will become the next shaman, it's like a fate worse than death. And the boy tries to run away and to escape, and it's the worst thing imaginable, because he'll be wounded in some way–in a psychological sense–and it's through that wound that the unconscious will be channeled. The sacred world will come through that wound, through that hole inside of him.

Selby: *Yeah.* Boy, does that sound accurate. *Wow.*

Couteau: You can relate to that?

Selby: Oh, dear Lord. Yes, indeed.

* * *

Couteau: What's your parents' background? Are you Irish?

Selby: No, English. Hundreds and hundreds and hundreds of years: all English.

Couteau: On each side?

Selby: Yeah, my family on both sides has been in this country for more than 350 years.

Couteau: They were probably the last English family left in Bay Ridge!

Selby: I was a member of the smallest minority in the country, for God's sake! [laughs] *I want minority rights*, God bless us! [laughs]

Couteau: You're working on an autobiography now?

Selby: No, not really. I was writing a memoir. I wanted to put down as much information as possible about myself for my children. Because I realized: who the heck can know their parents? Even if you have a whole bunch of facts. I know nothing about my father, not even the facts or anything else. But who can really know them? When you're a kid, they're God: they're all this; they're that. I just thought it would be nice to leave a document for my children where they can see the humanness inside of their father. It's not finished, because I've got so many other things happening. Suddenly, I was writing *The Willow Tree*, and now something else. Also, I was writing a thing called "Seeds of Pain, Seeds of Love" that is very autobiographical. I don't know if I'll ever get back and organize that and finish it. It's just ... I never know.

Couteau: I understand that you're currently working on a book that deals with the theme of suicide.

Selby: Well, not really suicide. What the theme is ... it's hard for me to say, because this thing evolved from a joke, just like *Requiem for a Dream* evolved from a joke. It might be, simply, having a purpose in life.

The thing started: this guy is very despondent; he's very unhappy. So he's trying to figure out how to kill himself. And eventually he decides he's going to–this is a long thing–but finally he decides he's going to get a gun and blow his brains out. And so he goes to get a gun, and they need information to okay it: you know, to get a permit, whatever it's called. And the computer system breaks down, and he has to wait five days. He becomes pissed off at all this, and in that five-day period he goes from being suicidal to homicidal. So he figures: oh, he'll kill this guy at the Veteran's Administration who's been breaking his balls.

He doesn't want to just murder him; he wants to make it

look natural, so he doesn't have to pay a price. So he goes on the Internet, and he finds out how to culture E. coli and salmonella bacteria. And to make a long story short, he drops it in the guy's Coke one day at lunch, and the guy actually dies. And he goes and he visits the body, and he's really delighted over this, really happy: *"I killed a man; I killed a man!"*

And then, of course, he's even more depressed than ever. And he sits around for about three days with the gun barrel in his mouth, hoping that if he can't pull the trigger maybe he'll fall down and accidentally pull the trigger. So then the TV is on, and suddenly something captures his ear.

They're talking about the thirtieth picnic and barbecue celebration in some place, and you get the distinct impression that it's Mississippi. What it's about is: thirty years before, when they were integrating the hospitals for Medicare. The doctors were going all over the country doing this. And there was a black doctor working in this particular town, and he was murdered. And everyone knew that this guy had done it. Then they brought him to trial, and they found him not guilty. And everyone celebrated right after the trial with a barbecue and picnic. And every year since then, they have this barbecue and picnic celebration. So this guy–"Ah, ha!"–now he has a purpose to his life, see?

So he's going to get this guy. And he'll get this guy in the same E. coli kind of manner. But then what he'll do is: he's going to see if he can start a mafia war between different gangs and have them eliminate each other. He's going to go around–I don't know how many: three, four different cities–and blow up some mafia people, hoping they'll all start shooting each other and all that kind of thing.

Couteau: You're currently working on this?
Selby: Yeah.
Couteau: What about writing in the first person? When I read the little that's available about your biography, it seems that it would be a natural thing for you to write in the first person. Is your memoir in the first person?

Selby: Oh, well, yeah. And this "Waiting Period" thing that I just told you about, the suicide guy, that's first person. There's actually no narrator. There's actually no narrator at all.

Couteau: It's first person?

Selby: Yeah. It's all inside this guy's head, like in *The Room*. There's no narrator, but there is a commentator that kind of pops up, every now and then. Sometimes he seems to be the devil, and sometimes he seems to be Jesus. I don't know who he is. He just pops in and out. And makes comments about things.

Couteau: Maybe back to that thing about the two sides, the two faces, right?

Selby: Yeah, who knows? [laughs]

Couteau: It seems to me that would be a natural thing for you to do, given the incredible life ... you know, you've had a very rich life, and a very intense life. Is this the first time that you've had the impulse to write in the first person?

Selby: No, there are some things ...

Couteau: I know you have some short stories ...

Selby: Some stories are in the first person. And then, oh, that thing, the "Seeds of Pain, Seeds of Love," the autobiographical thing: that's first person. But I jump from first to third. I do that a lot in all my work; I'm sure you've noticed.

Couteau: You listen to Beethoven every day and you've

mentioned Céline, who's a very musical writer. When you're writing, do the words come in rhythm or melody?

Selby: Yeah. Depending upon what's needed. See, I always try to fulfill the responsibility to the story: whatever is needed at the moment. But yeah, I write by ear. Yeah, the rhythms of the writing, even in the narrative, are important. For instance, if I'm writing a narrative about a particular person, dealing with a particular person, the rhythms, the syntax, and so forth, should reflect that person's personality.

Couteau: It was obvious to me that you were writing by ear; I just wanted to make sure. It's one of the reasons your writing is so beautiful, and so different, from many other writers.

Just a couple of last questions. Are there any nonfiction writers or books that were a big influence?

Selby: Well, maybe when I was ... when I was a kid, I did read one book. And that was called *Heroes of Science*. And it had Edward Jenner, Lavoisier, and, oh, I can't remember the various scientists. But I do remember reading that book. And I remember, when I was eight or ten years old, making a decision that I was going to find a way to stop the suffering in the world. [laughs]

Couteau: Well, that's interesting!

Selby: [laughs] Yes, indeed. I think about that now. And, you know, I think about it, and it really wasn't an ego trip. It wasn't like, "*I'm* going to do this."

Couteau: It wasn't coming out of a power complex.

Selby: No, it was a real sincere thing. I was that kind of kid. I guess I had, by that time, seen enough suffering. And I just really wanted people to stop hurting each other.

Couteau: You said that you don't know much about your dad. I imagine that your mom must have been an incredible influence.

Selby: Yeah. They were both very, very influential. My mother's a very strong, powerful woman. And my father was a drunk. He died drunk at the age of seventy-eight, so it wasn't like a premature death. And I've just cloned myself after my father. Oh, in so many ways. Violent, drunk, maniacal. I left home and went to sea, and he went to sea. And oh, just ... oh, all that kind of stuff. But at the same time, my mother was a reader. But she just couldn't stand bad language! [laughs] I used to get a bar of lye soap in my mouth for using words like *lousy*.

Couteau: Wow!

Selby: [laughs] Oh, boy! But at the same time, she got me to museums periodically. At least a couple of times a year we went to museums, things of that nature. My father went back to sea in 1942, and I always had a part-time job after school or before school, whichever. Which meant that I used to work a half day Saturday, and quite often we'd meet, go to a movie. And once we saw *Othello*, with Paul Robeson. Oh! Boy, what an experience that was! And so, there was a balance.

You know, as we've said, there are no absolutes. There was a lot of conflict. I wanted to please my mother, and I wanted to please my father. And so, [laughs] it's pretty hard to please them both when they were so opposite in personality. So, I was always caught up in this conflict.

Couteau: Was your father kind to you? Was he loving to you?

Selby: Well, not overtly. I realize now that he felt so incredibly inadequate. He didn't know what the hell to do.

You know, there's one thing I do know about him. He was twelve years old; he was all alone in the world and working in a coal mine. So you know, that's not exactly a great background to bring to a marriage.

Couteau: His parents were both ...

Selby: Dead. Yeah.

Couteau: They died at about that time or ...

Selby: Well, first his mother died when he was very young. He comes from Island, Kentucky. And then, when he was about twelve, I guess, his father died, and his stepmother just packed up and left. So, he went to live with an aunt in Indiana and worked in the coal mines. And he was just a little guy.

Couteau: He was confronted with a whole lot of reality very early on.

Selby: Oh, yeah! Right.

Couteau: And your mother, I would imagine, was more overt with her affection?

Selby: Oh, yeah, with her affection. And she sang in the same choir for more than sixty years. She'd still be there, but she can't get out of bed.

Couteau: How old is she now?

Selby: She's eighty-nine.

Couteau: What does she think of your work? What was her reaction?

Selby: Well, I'll tell you, man. Her reaction to *Last Exit* was one of the greatest compliments I've ever gotten. Because I told you her thing about language.

Couteau: Okay! So if *lousy* was a bad word, what did she think of *Last Exit*?

Selby: Well, she read the book, and this is what she said. She said: "Oh, those poor people." Wow. So, I mean, I *really* must have succeeded in doing what I planned to do. And that is: to put the reader through an emotional experience, because the experience of reading that book transcended all her prejudices, her ideas, her beliefs, and she just responded to the pain of the people.

Couteau: That must have been the ultimate compliment.

Selby: Oh! It's the greatest compliment that I've gotten. Absolutely. Oh, yeah. Because I know how she feels. [laughs] You know what I mean?

Couteau: Has she read your subsequent books?

Selby: I've given her a copy of each one. I don't know if she's actually read them all. I don't know if she was able to get through *The Room*. Some people can't.

Couteau: I think it's one of your best.

Selby: I think it's the most disturbing book ever written by a human being. But I think it's a masterpiece.

Couteau: Is that your own favorite, of all your work?

Selby: Well, I can't say it's a favorite. In one sense it is, because ... after I finished writing that thing, I stayed away from it for twelve years. It was really disturbing. And then I went back to it, and I was just delighted. Because, in *Last Exit*, I was struggling so hard to learn how to write. Oh, God, I can't describe to you the pain and torture: every night, for six years, trying to learn how to write. And so, I'm so involved in it that I can't see what I'm learning. But in rereading *The Room* all those years later, I could see so clearly how, in *Last Exit*, I had learned how to write. Because I learned how to put down a simple line–that is so simple, and so obvious, and that, hopefully, contains a certain degree of profundity.

Couteau: You were channeling the creative will in a much easier way.

Selby: Yeah. And I had acquired tools and techniques that I could utilize whenever the need arose. I could see that when I reread *The Room*. I think it's a remarkable book. I really do.

Couteau: I agree with you. What's incredible about that book is its minimal beauty. The setting is a single room. The "characters" are just one person. The dialogue is a monologue. Were those intentional things or was that just something that evolved?

Selby: The basic premise of the book was totally musical: variations on a theme. And I wanted it just as simple, as simple, as simple as possible.

Couteau: Was there any particular thing that inspired that idea, that concept to create a sort of minimal masterpiece?

Selby: It grew out of a story called "The Sound." I don't know if you remember that story or not.

Couteau: Is it in *Song of the Silent Snow*?

Selby: Yeah. A guy is locked in a cell, and he hears a strange noise. And he's looking out, and he becomes scared and so forth. Turns out, he's having DTs [delirium tremens]. But that's where that originated. That was the germ of the idea for *The Room*.

Couteau: I understand you were actually locked up for a month.

Selby: Yeah. That's where they both come from.

Couteau: Was that the germ for the short story then?

Selby: Yeah. As a matter-of-fact, I wrote that in jail. I was in solitary a month, and then I was in population for a month.

Couteau: Why did they put you in solitary? Because you

were detoxing?

Selby: Yeah. And because ... This wasn't solitary, like in the hole. This was, you know, a single occupancy room, an *SRO!* [laughs uproariously] Because of my tubercular history, I was put in isolation, I guess. So I had this single-room-occupancy cell. [laughs]

Couteau: My astrologer friends made me promise to ask if you know what time you were born.

Selby: Oh, dear, I don't know. I think it was something like 11:00 a.m. And that would be New York time. But I'm not certain about that.

Couteau: I remember reading, years ago, in the *Village Voice* that, because of your health problems, you turned to astrology. Is that true?

Selby: No. What happened was: when I was very young, we lived in a luxury building. My father was the super: 59 West 12. Across the street from where the New School is now. It wasn't there at the time. But it was a luxury building. And there was an older lady in there that really took a liking to me. I was maybe three years old when we lived there, or four. And she had my horoscope drawn up by somebody that I've been told is a very famous astrologer: Alan Leo.*

Couteau: Yeah. He's from an older generation of astrologers.

Selby: Yeah, I guess he would be, because this was maybe 1931 or '32 that it was drawn up. And what happened is: many, many years later, I found, I came across this. I had it, and I read it. So, I never had one made up.

Couteau: Was it accurate?

Selby: Well, yeah, there are some interesting things. Like: "Stay away, be careful about going to sea," and stuff like that. [laughs]

Couteau: Really, he said that?

Selby: Yeah! [laughs] "Be careful of things like alcohol and drugs."

Couteau: And "Be careful if you leave your house. Better to stay at home!"

Selby: Yeah! [laughs] And you know, "You might want to look into the arts." Things like that.

Couteau: Actually, he's a very respected astrologer. He's published quite a bit.

Selby: Yeah. But it doesn't say on there about what time I was born. So, that's why I couldn't really say. And it's got all these figures. I guess these … not illustrations …

Couteau: The glyphs for the signs?

Selby: Glyphs! Yeah. Those things for the different months and stuff. So, I don't know what's what.

Couteau: Obviously, you're a spiritual man, and you've developed a philosophy that comes out of spiritual experience. Was there a point in your life when that started to happen? Was there something in particular that occurred?

Selby: Well, boy ... You know, when you start looking back on your life, you see it happening all along. But the big thing, *the* big thing was: thirty years ago, I stopped drinking. And that gave me a chance to get in touch with, shall we say, my own reality, as far as this world is concerned. *Very* uncomfortable! [laughs] But that, of course, was the big thing.

But I can look back on things that are just remarkable. We had a little thing called "Poetry in Motion" out here. We had poetry readings every week for about four years.

And the fun part of it was that each week they'd have a topic. Just some arbitrary thing. You know, like "fashion," "passion," "terminal cool," "it takes one to know one," you know, "sports heroes," that kind of stuff. And then you'd write something around this topic.

So I wrote a thing about what happened when I was about eighteen years old in the hospital. And what it was: this old guy, Hocus Pocus, he was a little old Estonian guy; we used to kind of make fun of him because he was a religious man. And he had this very deep affection for this young Greek boy. He was probably still in his teens, too; he was a Greek from Egypt. And he was going for his routine operation. Every three weeks, he got another three ribs cut out. It was one of those things. And he went for his first operation, and he didn't come back for a while, and ... Well, anyway, it turned out, he died.

So, this old guy, Hocus Pocus, was really broken up over this. And one day he came over to my bed, and he asked me to write him a letter. Now, I never wrote a letter in my life; I didn't know from nothing. And I said yes. I guess I was just moved by his need. So he said he wanted to write a letter to Alex's–that was the boy's name–Alex's parents, and to say that he was a good boy, and that we're sorry.

So, I don't know, somehow, I wrote a letter and it met with his liking. And we mailed it. And then we got a *reply* back. And the parents said they were so happy to hear from us and that sort of thing. And they exchanged a few letters. And then I realized, as I was writing this (and I wrote this forty years after the fact), two things:

First, in the story itself, I say: why did this guy ask *me* to do this? There were plenty of people in this ward who were better qualified; *everybody* was better qualified than I was.

In addition to that, they had Gray Ladies* there, social service … anybody ... but he asked me. And the conclusion I came up with … and this only happened as I'm writing, see; that's why I say that I don't know what I have to give until I'm in the process of giving it away–as I'm writing this thing, on the paper it says: "Because I was in more need of the miracle he was offering than anybody else."

And because I had said *yes* to life, I found out that I always have within me the infinite resources necessary to fulfill my responsibility at the moment. And what he was giving me was the gift of love. The gift that I could love. And then, later on, I realized–and again, this is maybe forty-two years after the fact–*that* is where I made the decision to be a writer. Now, I know that, absolutely. Now I may be talking about a spiritual decision, but that is where it really originated. I said *yes* to writing a letter.

Couteau: It's very interesting, because my question was about spiritual experience, and you immediately focused on your role as a writer.

Selby: Mm-hmm. Right.

Couteau: So in a sense, this is your spiritual *raison d'être*: what you're doing, what you do.

Selby: I believe so. But see, I believe the first thing that I mentioned was that he gave me the gift of love. That's the first thing I recognized. The gift of love. That I could commit a loving act. And that was vitally important to me, because I thought I was the lowest form of animal life in the world. I was totally incapable of loving. And I wanted to be loving more than anything: more than I wanted life itself. And it tortured me …

Couteau: Your own judgments?

Selby: Of myself.

Couteau: The way that you looked at yourself?

Selby: Yeah.

Couteau: As a result of the illness?

Selby: No, just a result of everything. I always felt that way, all my life. I just ... and there's no reason for it: no reason, in fact. I just thought I was evil.

Couteau: And you don't know why?

Selby: No. Just ... the way it is.

Couteau: You know, when we read things about you, writers always sort of draw this vertical line: Before the illness; after the illness. Do you feel that? Or do you feel something else that is a continuity, which is not separated in that way? I mean, did it *fundamentally* change you?

Selby: Oh, yeah. Well, yes, absolutely.

Couteau: Your soul?

Selby: Well, no, I don't think it changed my soul. But it certainly changed my perception of it. And it changed my perception of my place in this world. See, I had no education; I left home at fifteen. And when I was a kid, I was a very physical kid. I was maybe six feet tall, 170 pounds. I was just a physical kid. And now, all of a sudden, I have all these ribs removed. I'm just devastated. The physical world is no longer my friend. I can't function in the physical world. And I am terrified. Now, let me tell you something I just remembered that's indicative of the opinion I had of myself.

When I was finally brought back to this country, they said I was going to die. They didn't tell me; they told my mother. And they had me in this little, itty-bitty room. It was just big enough for the bed. They just stick you in there to die. When I was in there, I couldn't lie down. I had to sit up in bed all the time, because I couldn't breathe. And it was like, I gasped for air. You know, always gasping. And I remember so clearly the thought that just went through my head. It was: God put me here in order to atone for all my sins.

Now, what in the hell kind of an opinion did I have of me?

Couteau: Where did that come from?

Selby: Don't ask me!

Couteau: No idea?

Selby: No. But that's the opinion I had of me. That I'm just ... I'm really ... And I told this to a shrink once. And then he asked me, he says, "Well, what did you do that was so terrible that you deserved to die like that, at the age of eighteen?" And I lay there a while [laughs]–I had no answer! Finally–this is so insane, when I think about it–the only answer I could come up with, after *many* minutes of thinking, was: I quit school. Now, isn't that insane? That's the kind of thing I'm working with internally! [laughs] I quit school. But I mean, if you know the whole background, it does make a little sense. Because my parents wanted me to be happy. They wanted me to go to school, get a good job, and so forth. And I left school. And that hurt them. So, in a sense, it does make some sense. But still, that's really crazy.

Couteau: You describe yourself as being a very empathetic child and adult. And this is what I feel, even when I read *Last Exit*, which, as you've said somewhere else, you said something like: There is no light in this book. And the reader is forced to turn to his own light, you know, *inside*.

Selby: Mm-hmm. Yeah. He has no relief.

Couteau: There's no relief in that book. Except maybe in that story, "And Baby Makes Three," which I think is a fun story.

Selby: [laughs] Well, yeah. And that was there just for that reason. I put it right there just because I had the sense that, if I don't change the tempo of the music, the rest can start to become a monotone and lose its power.

Couteau: I see. But again, when I read *Last Exit*, there's an authorial presence; your presence is in the book, and we feel it during those brief moments of empathy when, for example, Georgette imagines a different world ...

Selby: Mm-hmm.

Couteau: ... a wonderful, loving world. And there are other characters, in other moments in the book, through which that occurs. Was that an intentional part of what you tried to do in *Last Exit*? Or was it just that you were sort of "leaking" into the book?

Selby: Well, it must just be "leaking," because I never wanted me to be in there in any way whatsoever. But as I said, I put the reader through an emotional experience. I have to write from the inside out. And it seemed absolutely essential that that romantic image, which can be so lyrical within Georgie and, at the same time, so deadly, be expressed.

Couteau: Because it's part of the human condition.

Selby: Yeah.

Couteau: And you're writing about the human condition.

Selby: That's right.

Couteau: Well, Mr. Selby, this has been an emotional catharsis for me, talking to you!

Selby: [laughs]

Couteau: I really want to thank you for your time.

Selby: Well, thank you! It's been a very interesting interview. You asked some really interesting questions. It was a lot of fun.

Couteau: Thank you. What did the guys in Brooklyn think when you published *Last Exit*? Did any of them read it?

Selby: Well, a couple of them read at least part of *Last Exit*. And [imitating a Brooklyn accent]: "Say, man, this ain't the way it was!" [laughs]

Couteau: They said that?

Selby: Yeah, they all said the same thing! [laughs]

Couteau: Were they just giving you a hard time?

Selby: No, no! It's just, you know: poetic license! I mean, it's based on my experiences in life, but: "It's not the way it happened." [laughs]

Couteau: Were any of the stories in *Last Exit* things that actually occurred?

Selby: Well, yeah, a little bit. "And Baby Makes Three": it was kind of ... that sort of happened, at least part of it. There was a time when somebody was fucking around with a knife and stabbed Georgie.

Couteau: Georgie really existed?

Selby: Oh, yeah, Georgie's very real. What else? There was a strike.

Couteau: That's an amazing story, "Strike." It really makes you feel as if you're inside a little Brooklyn office somewhere.

Selby: I mean, the strike was real, but everything else, of course, was just pure imagination. "Tralala": there was a person named Tralala. I never saw her. That's the only connection with reality, the name.

Couteau: Two last things that pop into my head: let me throw these at you. Why is there so much homosexuality–you know, the drag queens–in *Last Exit*? Why does it happen so frequently? And the other question I wanted to ask: you were saying that you felt as if you were at the bottom rung of humanity. How do you feel about yourself now?

Selby: Oh, I've come to terms with all that. Mostly, by correcting the errors I've made on the outside: doing all I can to compensate for any pain and misery I've caused people. And through these experiences that we've talked about, I get a greater glimmer of my reality. So, I just don't believe the lies that go through my head anymore. The homosexuality really stems from just Georgie, for one thing. And there is this connection through it so that the guy in "Strike" is actually going out with people that were introduced to him through Georgie. So, that's just the thread. It's not ...

Couteau: It's just the thread that runs through the book then.

Selby: Yeah. It's not that there's so much homosexuality, although it may appear that way. It starts with Georgie, who's a neighborhood kid. And then he brings around some of the others, and that kind of thing. Also, you must remember that most of these guys that we're talking about here, and writing about, had been in the joint for a while. So, fucking young boys in the ass is S.O.P.

Couteau: What's S.O.P.?

Selby: Standard Operational Procedure.

Couteau: [laughs] That's true. You even use the word "con" at some point in the book. You say, "a bunch of cons." And someone "had never hung out with cons before": one of the girls.

Selby: Yeah, right. I remember once seeing a couple–two males–on a subway, many years ago. And this one guy had a real typical Irish ex-con look. And he was big. And he just had that look. And he had this frail looking little guy with him, and they were holding hands, you know. But nobody was going say anything! [laughs]

Couteau: Nobody was going to fuck with him, right?

Selby: [laughs] *No* way!

Couteau: By the way, it's interesting that you're using some Internet stuff in your latest book. I mean, that's something we'd never expect in a Hubert Selby book.

Selby: Well, I figured: where else is he going to find that? It seems everybody's got a Net, an Internet thing.

Couteau: That's a great idea.

Selby: Yeah, so …

Couteau: Is living in L.A. changing your writing in any way, or what you're writing about?

Selby: Well, you'd have to answer that. I mean, has it? I don't think so ...

Couteau: I meant, for example, are there any L.A. characters or ... Well, I guess you're still writing about New York, obviously ...

Selby: Uh-huh. I think I still write with … whatever power I have is still there, I believe.

Couteau: I just meant in terms of something you might experience in L.A. that you would never experience in New York and that eventually finding its way into your writing.

Selby: Who knows? It's possible. Well, the guy with the suicide-murder thing, I guess that could be L.A., why not?

Couteau: What was the origin of "Psalm 16"? That has to be one of your most incredible short pieces. I was telling my friends that, when I die, I want the priest to read it at my funeral!

Selby: [laughs] Really? Well, that was those poetry readings I was telling you about. And the theme one night was "Song of Forgiveness." And this is what I ended up writing. A song of forgiveness.

I'll tell you something interesting about that. I sent a copy to my mother. She was still ambulatory at the time, so it must have been like ten years ago. And she showed it to her pastor in her church. And he wrote to me asking if he could have a copy of it to use. He said, "I never read religious literature, because it's just too easy. But *you* ask *hard*

questions." [laughs] So, he was fascinated by it.

Couteau: That's an amazing little story.

Selby: Yeah, isn't it?

Couteau: It really is, yeah. Of course, he'll probably never read it at the church but, still, it's a great story!

Selby: [laughs]

Couteau: I was reading van Gogh's letters the other day, and I noticed that Vincent sent a copy of one of his sermons to his brother Theo.

Selby: Yeah, Vincent was a preacher up there in the Belgian coal mines for a while. He was a religious fanatic. He just couldn't come to terms with it. You know, God is love–and look at the suffering. It was ... *whew*. Oh, who can come to terms with that?

Couteau: It's one of those questions that will always haunt mankind.

Selby: Mm-hmm. Yeah, as long as we have that personalized God.

From a two-hour phone interview conducted between Los Angeles and Paris on 20 September 1999. An abridged version was featured in *Rain Taxi Review of Books* (online) in December 1999.

* Although *Tropic of Cancer* was published by Grove Press in 1961, it wasn't until June 22, 1964 that the U.S. Supreme Court ruled the book to be not obscene. In Florida and Philadelphia, however, litigation continued until 1966.
* An American television comedy about a journalist named Murphy Brown, which aired from 1988 to 1998. After "Murphy" decided to raise a child as a single parent, Vice President Dan Quayle denounced her for "ignoring the importance of fathers by birthing a child alone."
* This is actually a line from Ezra Pound: "Artists are the antennae of the race."
* Leo died in 1917, so Selby must have had someone else in mind.
*Red Cross workers, who wore gray uniforms.

The Romance of Places:
An Interview with Ray Bradbury

One of the most well known writers of science fiction and the recipient of numerous awards for his stories and screenplays, Ray Bradbury's books include The Martian Chronicles, The Illustrated Man, *and* Fahrenheit 451. *Bradbury was also the Idea Consultant for the United States Pavilion at the 1964 World's Fair and has worked as a consultant on city engineering and rapid transit.*

A frequent visitor to Paris, especially to the restaurants and bookshops in the Latin Quarter, he claims to have fallen in love with it all thirty-seven years ago when he first arrived here, to work with John Huston on the screenplay of Moby Dick. *Seated in the lobby of the Hotel Normandy near the Palais Royal, he spoke of his fascination with Paris and of his other passions, such as city planning, his method of writing, and the future of science fiction.*

Couteau: My first question concerns the process of writing. Do you have any sort of daily ritual that serves as a preparation to writing, or do you just sit down every day at a certain time and begin?

Bradbury: Well, the ritual is waking up, number one, and then lying in bed and listening to my voices. Then, over a period of years ... I call it my morning theater; it's inside my head. And my characters talk to one another, and when it reaches a certain pitch of excitement, I jump out of bed and run and trap them before they are gone. So, I never have to worry about a routine; they're always in there, talking.

Couteau: How long do you write for?

Bradbury: Oh, a couple of hours. You can do three or four thousand words and that's more than enough for one day.

Couteau: How has the use of the computer affected your writing?

Bradbury: Not at all, because I don't use it.

Couteau: You never use a computer?

Bradbury: I can write faster on a typewriter than you can on a computer. I do 120 words a minute, and you can't do that on a computer. So, I don't need anything … That's plenty fast.

Couteau: So you're saying the technology still hasn't caught up with you.

Bradbury: Well, if it won't be any more efficient than my IBM Selectric, why should I buy it? It's for corrections, you know? Then I give it to my daughter, and she has a computer and she puts it in, and she then corrects it in the computer. And we have a record, so we have the best of both worlds at the same time.

Couteau: How about the imaginative process itself, the building of a story? How do characters and plots first arise? You've maybe covered this a little just now. Do they appear spontaneously or do they first originate in a carefully planned conscious construct?

Bradbury: Any carefully planned thing destroys the creativity. You can't think your way through a story; you have to live it. So, you don't build a story; you allow it to explode.

Couteau: Do you, for instance, use people and places out of the past, out of your own life?

Bradbury: Very rarely. More recently, yes, in my two murder mysteries, *Death Is a Lonely Business* and the sequel, which just came out, *A Graveyard for Lunatics*. Events in my past life are in there: some people that I knew. But most of my stories are ideas in action. In other words, I get a concept, and I let it run away. I find a character to act out the idea. And then the story takes care of itself.

Couteau: Certain modern writers, such as William Burroughs, have used characters and settings first observed in dream states as the basis for fictional experiments. Others, such as Henry Miller, have spoken of being "dictated to" by the unconscious …

Bradbury: That sounds more like my cup of tea …

Couteau: Have you had similar experiences with what might be termed non-ego influences on the creative imagination? I mean there are others: drugs or meditation or whatever. Or dreams.

Bradbury: No, dreams don't work. And I don't know of anyone that ever wrote anything based on dreams constantly. You may get inspiration once every ten years. But dreams are supposed to function to cure you of some problem that you have, so you leave those alone. That's a different process. But the morning process when you're waking up, and you're half-asleep and half-awake: that's the perfect time. Because then you're relaxed, and the brain is floating between your ears. It's not attached. Or getting in the shower, first thing in the morning, when your body is totally relaxed and your mind is totally relaxed. You're not thinking; you're intuiting. And then the little explosions, the little revelations come. Or taking a nap in the afternoon. It's the same state. But you can't force things. People try to force things. It's disastrous. Just leave your mind alone.

Your intuition knows what it wants to write, so get out of the way.

Couteau: Where did you fly in from?

Bradbury: From New York City. But I'm from Los Angeles.

Couteau: New York's my hometown.

Bradbury: Well, it's a good place to get away from. It's a shame. Because I've been going there since I was nineteen, and I've watched the whole thing go to hell. I had a lot of friends there. And I love the Metropolitan Museum and the Guggenheim. But I mean, how much love can you have for something? The only livable place is down on Pier 17: South Street Seaport. Have you ever been down there? It's great. And it's very social. It's very safe. A lot of good restaurants. And I go up to this restaurant facing the Brooklyn Bridge: Harbor Lights. A lot of wonderful Irishmen run the place. And I go up and get drunk with them. I lived a year in Ireland. So, we get on very well. We talk about the Royal Hibernian Hotel and things like that.

Couteau: You've been the recipient of numerous book awards. You've been received by world leaders such as Mikhail Gorbachev. When the *Apollo* astronauts landed on the moon, they paid you homage by naming the Dandelion Crater in honor of your novel, *Dandelion Wine*. How has this overall acceptance by people in positions of great responsibility affected your writing and your life?

Bradbury: Not at all. You just don't think about it; you shouldn't. The most dangerous thing you can do is know who you are. See, Norman Mailer's problem is he thinks he's Norman Mailer. And Gore Vidal's problem is he thinks he's Gore Vidal. I don't think I'm Ray Bradbury. So, there's a big difference. Just do your work every day; don't go around thinking, "Gee," you know, "wow!" To hell with that. The work is important; the work is fun. And there's no time. If you get into your work every day, there's no time to think who you are. So … these are very nice things, and I was exhilarated by them when they happened. My day with Gorbachev was joyous, and I went home immensely happy. But then the next day, you've got things to do. So, it hasn't affected me at all.

Couteau: I'm curious about your vision of the future. I'm thinking now of a story that first appeared in the early 1950s: "The Pedestrian." In this rather paranoid vision of the future, a Mr. Meade is arrested and sent to a psychiatric center for having committed the transgression of walking, without a purpose, through the streets at night. It's a world in which magazines and books don't sell anymore and people sit in rooms mesmerized by television sets. In many ways, this tale epitomizes the very dark undercurrent of the 1950s. Yet there are forces at work in the world today that are not that dissimilar. What about your personal vision of the future, especially the political future?

Bradbury: Well, it's very optimistic. Look what's happened in the last eight months. Because America stood firm, and helped form NATO, and just stayed quietly there, finally, the Communists gave up. They *were* an evil empire; you know, Reagan was absolutely right. And they partially still are, because they haven't finished disarming.

But who could have foreseen that the end would have come so quickly? And within just a matter of months. We said, take down the wall. We implied it many times. Only one president ever said it: Reagan. He's not going to get any credit for it. Everyone hates him for being successful. He'll probably go down in history as the most important president of the century. Because he did in the Communist empire. Just by holding steady and being very quiet. And when the Communists left the negotiating table three or four years ago, everyone said, "Oh, President Reagan, don't do that," you know, "call them back." He said, "They'll be back. They have to come back. Because their economy isn't working, so if we just, if we're not belligerent, don't take advantage of it, don't rock the boat, they'll be back. And eventually, the Wall will come down." And that's exactly what happened. So, two weeks ago, the Russians welcomed Reagan to Moscow, huh? Because he helped them get free of their own system. It's ironic. It's beautiful. And the one president we thought would never be able to do this is the one who did it.

Couteau: How about the opening of the East Bloc? How will that affect science-fiction writing?

Bradbury: I don't think it will affect it much. Because we're running ahead of all that. We've always talked about freedom; we've always talked about totalitarian governments. After all, *Fahrenheit 451* is all about Russia, and all about China, isn't it? And all about the totalitarians anywhere: either left or right, doesn't matter where they are; they're book burners, all of them. And so, *Fahrenheit* will continue to be a read book, by people all over the world. Because there are still totalitarian governments. And book burners. So as long as that's true, or if the threat is true, the book will be read.

Couteau: This past August you celebrated your seventieth birthday. After devoting decades of your life to writing science fiction, have you arrived at any conclusion concerning the function of science fiction, either in our individual lives or in the life of the social collective?

Bradbury: Well, it's the most important fiction ever invented; it always has been. People haven't given it credit. Because it has to do with the history of ideas. Of dreaming an idea, birthing an idea, blueprinting an idea, making it into a fact. And then moving on, to the next idea.

The history of science fiction started in the caves 20,000 years ago. The ideas on the walls of the cave were problems to be solved. It's problem solving. Primitive scientific knowledge, primitive dreams, primitive blueprinting: to solve problems. I never really realized how honorable and how long the history of science fiction is. You look on the walls of the caves: they had pictures of antelopes, and gazelles, and mammoths. And the problem there is: how do you kill them? And that's a science-fiction problem, isn't it? You have to think of it first before you can solve it. Then you find ways of inventing knives and then spears. A spear is an extension of a man's arm and his imagination. And when you throw it, you're throwing your will. You're throwing your arm, and you're killing the animal. So that's science-fiction dreaming becoming primitive fact. You finally find out how to kill animals. So you can survive. And then, how do you build a fire? That's science fiction, isn't it?

As soon as you pose the question, that's science fiction. Because you're *imagining* something and trying to figure out, "Gee, if we can bring fire to the cave ... but it goes out. We find it in the forest after the lightning strikes, and we grab it and bring it back, but, the next day, it's gone. How do you keep it forever?" So, you dream that, and then you solve it, and then you have science fact. Primitive science, huh? So, the whole history of mankind is survival.

Science-fiction dreaming science-factual finding. And then, moving on to the next problem.

How do you go to the moon, huh? Science fiction, just forty years ago. Impossible! I had to put up with people saying to me, when I was thirty: "We're never going to do that. Come on; don't be stupid. It's a silly thing to even think about. Why go to the moon? Why go to Mars?" Well, all of a sudden, just a few years ago, we solved the problem. So, the science-fictional dream became the *Apollo* missions. So now, we're dreaming of what? We're dreaming of landing men on the moon. We're dreaming of going out to the other planets, with manned missions eventually, sometime in the next forty or fifty years. Probably land on Mars sometime in the next twenty years. And look at the Hubble Telescope. I take it that it's beginning to function now. That's a dream that goes a long way back: a long way back. And it was totally impossible. It was science fiction. Now it's out there, looking at the stars. Eventually, we'll go to Proxima Centauri. That will be sometime in the next thousand years. Maybe even sooner. If we can make our rockets go half the speed of light, we can get out there in eight or ten years. And that's not bad. Anything longer than that is pretty hard on the human psyche, not to mention the human body.

And then, all the other things that have occurred. The invention of a Xerox machine, which is a printing press for every human being in the world. That's why they don't exist in Russia. All these technological things are freedoms in the United States, right now. Most people couldn't tell you how many airplanes there are, private airplanes. There are 900,000 aviators: private aviators. There are between 200,000 and 300,000 airplanes, private airplanes, owned by individuals, and 20,000 landing strips. That's a freedom, isn't it? You can go anywhere you want to go. The airplane doesn't exist in Russia. That's one freedom that's denied everyone. Because they're afraid if they had airplanes, they'd leave the country. And they have very few telephones. Because they don't believe in communication. That's a freedom. We have a telephone for every person in the country, in America. There are no automobiles in Russia. It has yet to be invented.*

Couteau: If they can afford them though, right?

Bradbury: Huh?

Couteau: You said we have a telephone for everyone in the country. Everyone who can afford a telephone.

Bradbury: Everyone has a telephone. Whether they can afford it or not. It's one of those things that people have, regardless of their income.

Couteau: Well, how about someone who is …You're answers are piquing my interest in other questions, of course

…

Bradbury: [laughs] Okay. No, there are some things that all poor people have, automatically. They have TV …

Couteau: Well, how about a homeless person in New York …

Bradbury: Well, no, that's another problem entirely, which has to do with our emptying the lunatic asylums twenty-five years ago. It was a big liberal movement, and a conservative movement, too, because we hated lunatic asylums; we hated the idea of them, and we had medicines which we thought were going to work, right? It was an honorable experiment, but it didn't work. So, those people are out there. Now we have to take them off the streets; we cannot leave them out there.

Couteau: I worked in a program in New York that was involved with trying to find housing and jobs for homeless mentally ill people. It was one of the few programs set up to solve that problem. And I did encounter many people who barely got by, who had a home but couldn't afford a telephone or couldn't afford clothing or other things that we all take for granted. And what I'm getting at, what I'm leading to is … you're talking a lot about the Soviet Union. I'm wondering about your feelings about totalitarian strains within the United States.

Bradbury: There are none.

Couteau: You don't feel there are any?

Bradbury: No. Of course not. Never have been. We're a free society; we've got television. We have radio. We have newspapers. We have the videocassette, which is coming into play. These are new freedoms.

Couteau: How about right-wing reactionary forces, like the Klan? Wouldn't you say that's a totalitarian strain?

Bradbury: No, those things exist on both sides. The left wing wants to burn certain books, too, but they don't. We don't allow them to. The *Huckleberry Finn* liberal groups have been against … but we have to oppose that.

Couteau: Well, that's what I'm getting at. Do any of your stories, do they just talk about … Something like "The Pedestrian," which to me, when I read it, I thought it was such a wonderful thing, because I thought it was universal. It was something that wasn't specifically about China or the Soviet Union, but it was about totalitarian forces that may exist within any individual …

Bradbury: Oh, yeah. Every single individual is that same thing. You are; I am. And we have to make sure that we don't misbehave. Well, look what happened with the

French Revolution. It started out honorably. And then it passed into the hands of the mob. And so, they decided to have revenge, and everyone got killed. And then they devoured themselves. Which is neither left nor right. It's just destruction.

Couteau: Your stories do speak, then, to these totalitarian strains that may exist within any individual.

Bradbury: Oh, everywhere. Us … but our record is clean compared to what's … I mean, China has burned millions of books in the last twenty years.

Couteau: How about our record not domestically but let's say some of our questionable policies in South America over the last hundred years. Do you think it's that clean?

Bradbury: We recognized that. I think most people have discussed it, and we're, here and there, trying to do something about it. So that we erase the memory of that. But it's not totalitarian in the sense of what Russia's done when they invade a country and they kill millions of people. We haven't done that.

Couteau: Do we want to erase the record or do we want to face the record?

Bradbury: I think we've faced it. We've got plenty of books on it. Our libraries are full of them. And plenty of newspapers to remind us of that.

*　　*　　*

Couteau: In many ways, Mr. Bradbury, I see you as–it's perhaps a silly term–but I see you as the granddaddy of science fiction …

Bradbury: [laughs] I've turned into one!

Couteau: And, you know, I mean that even if you were twenty-five or thirty–in essence!

Bradbury: [laughs]

Couteau: If you were to prophesize, what are some of the directions and problems that science-fiction writing will explore in the oncoming decades?

Bradbury: Well, we've already done a lot of it. I mean, Orwell was certainly a good example, and he'd had terrible personal adventures with Communism. And other people have had encounters with other kinds of totalitarian forces.

I think a lot of our thinking and writing in the next twenty or thirty years–at least mine will be–will be focused on the need to get us back into space again. Because we've allowed the *Challenger* to destroy our willpower. I mean, you know, it really is just a few people who were killed. I'm sorry they're dead. It was very hard on them. It's hard on their relatives. It's hard on our psyche. But if we allow it … See, what happened in the twenty-four hours, forty-eight hours following the explosion: that film was on the air a hundred times. Well, if you see a thing often enough, you begin to disbelieve in the future. Television is very dangerous. Because it repeats and repeats and repeats our disasters, instead of our triumphs.

Look at what happened two years ago with the grapes from South America. It was blown all out of proportion. Destroyed an industry. TV did that, not newspapers. What about poison apples, you know? Where the old witch, Meryl Streep, says, "Here's an apple that isn't poisoned."* And they destroy the apple industry. What about radon in the cellar? It's a panic a week. So, TV … The problem in a free society is: how do you control a thing that is supposed to be free? Can you say to them, "One hundred times is enough for the *Challenger*"? That we turn it off for a while? Because we see it still, every once in a while. In one of the news shows, I think it was on CNN recently, I saw repeated that air accident, at Dresden or Hamburg, where the jet crashed into the crowd and burned up a hundred people right in front of you. They put that on the air every night. So, the disaster inclination, the panic inclination of TV, is very dangerous. But I don't know what to do about it, except to set an example, and say, hey, you know. TV is so vivid, and it rams it down your eyeballs night after night. So, I guess all we can ask of the TV networks is a little discretion. So that we won't believe the end of the world was yesterday. And we stop doing things.

My final point is: we haven't been in space. We're finally going back. And it's taken years now. We're afraid to move. We're frozen. So, the job of the science-fiction writer … I've been down to Canaveral during the last month. I've had meetings with some NASA people. I want to build a set of bleachers there for 5,000 people, and with gantries, and Dolby sound and music, and my narration, poetry, what have you, and, every night at sunset, put on a light-and-sound show, like they do here, in Paris, at various buildings, or in London. To teach us the history of *Apollo*, with all its incredible intensity and passion and ability to move the soul, so that we can "reteach" ourselves how exciting the thing was and still can be. So that from the bottom of the pyramid, people pressure the Congress into lopping off some money from the military and putting it over into space travel.

That's always been the problem. The last twenty-five years, I've argued about this many times. That we spend so much on the military, and the damned stuff just sits there.

It was important at one time. Now that Russia's beginning to back off, I'm hoping that some of that money–and once the Gulf Crisis is over, God help us–will be put into space. Because we need something to lift us: we have a tendency … because we all watch the 6:00 local news. See, that's the really destructive news. Because it's all suicides, murders, rapes, funerals, and AIDS. About most of which we can't do anything. AIDS we can do something about. But the funerals we can't go to. The murders we didn't commit. We didn't have anything to do with the rapes. But that's rammed into your eyeballs every night.

I'm trying to get people to watch *McNeil/Lehrer*, who are responsible, informative, and nonpolitical. Very important: nonpolitical. David Brinkley on Sunday, with Sam Donaldson on the left, George Will on the right, Brinkley in between: you know what the labels are. And the more informative programs we can have, with no panic and no disaster every night, so that we have equilibrium in our society.

A lot of people have been looking at the news 365 nights a year. At the end of a year, you give up on the human race. I don't want happy endings. I don't want to be Laughing Boy Number One. On the other hand, I don't want to see people going around disbelieving in the future in a country that's one of the best. Done a lot of good things. We've been taking in 500,000 immigrants a year for thirty years now, and some years a million. Now we're going to up it again this next year. I mean, where in hell do people go in this world? They come here. They come to America, rather: not here. But they also come to France, because it's a place to survive: a good place to survive.

Couteau: A moment ago, you mentioned something about the need to be uplifted, and you used the word "soul." Is this the long-term function of science fiction or your vision of what we need in the future? Are you talking about a unifying spiritual vision?

Bradbury: Yeah, I try to write about it. My stories are warnings; they're not predictions. If they were predictions, I wouldn't do them. Because then I'd be part of the doom-ridden psychology. But every time I name a problem, I try to give a solution.

So not only have I talked about the future and the past, but I've been part of creating three malls in California: the Glendale Galleria; the Horton Plaza, in San Diego; and the Westside Pavilion, at Westwood Boulevard and Pico. In other words, the failure of cities is the failure of chambers of commerce and the failure of the mayors and the city councils, who don't understand what cities are. They're in for political power; they're not in to re-create the city and make it better for everyone. So my dream has been: if they won't do it, some sort of corporate effort has to do it.

And Disney is my hero; I knew him when he was alive. And he created a model, on one level: Disneyland, Disney World, EPCOT. They're all social. They're not cities, but they give you examples of ways of living. Of lots of trees, lots of flowers. Lots of fountains and ponds, lots of places to sit, lots of places to eat, so that you can get out of the house again. In a lot of cities, people can't get out of the house; they're not safe. So a mall is an environment which is safe and beautiful–it can be–and creative and filled with examples of ways of living, like you find in the Latin Quarter here, over by Notre-Dame. Those mazes of restaurants: 200 of them, 300, 400. So, I'm trying to introduce that into American culture: to give people a chance to walk with their families, like down on Pier 17, and be social, and to be happy, instead of being afraid, walking through the streets of New York.

Hollywood Boulevard is a disaster. I'm trying to help them rebuild that. Parts of downtown L.A., I have plans for that, if the city mayor would only listen. But he's a big jerk, and he's trying to build an immigrant monument, which is stolid and massive and nothing, when we need something fluid to connect the areas of the city so the people can leave their cars behind and walk for miles, as you do in Paris here. You don't dream of driving. I mean if you do … I was trying to get here tonight; I was across town playing some tapes; it took me forty-five minutes just to come about a mile to get here. I could've walked it faster, and next time I will.

So, again: to give people back their feet, to give back their freedom, should be the job of the cities, except they don't know how to do it, and we science-fiction writers know. I know, and I criticized Century City in Los Angeles. Twenty years ago, they built two new cities, next to each other, and they interviewed me, and I said they won't work. And don't build them that way. And I said, you don't have enough restaurants. You have to have forty restaurants; you have to have a thousand tables, a thousand parasols, 4,000 chairs, spread all throughout this area, so that people can sit. It's a Mediterranean climate, California; it's beautiful! Three hundred days a year, you can sit out.

They didn't listen to me. Ten years later, disaster: both cities weren't working. They called me again and said, "We want an interview." I said, "If you let me tear your skin off, I'll do it." So, they printed everything I said. And I repeated: *Restaurants, restaurants, restaurants* are the secret of cities. People want to eat. And then, after they've eaten, they shop. They don't go out to shop; they go out to eat. They think they're going out to shop, but, really, they're going out to eat.

And once you do that, the whole soul is aerated. Your ambience changes. And walking around Paris, gee, you turn any corner, there are seven restaurants. And little shops. And millions of people on the street every night.

So, the social life here is incredible. And Disney was influenced by France. And I try to teach people at home: do what Disney did. He came here: time and again. He sent his best co-workers here, to study at the Sorbonne.

Couteau: Is that why you're in Paris so often?

Bradbury: Well, I fell in love with it on my own, thirty-seven years ago. I arrived here in 1953 to write the screenplay of *Moby Dick*, for John Huston. So this is where I met him, at the rue d'Athènes, and then we moved over to Ireland, and I lived there for seven months, finishing the screenplay. But every time I kept coming back and coming back, and now I spend every summer here, and this is my fourth trip this year. My wife's arriving tomorrow night; she loves it as much as I do.

Couteau: So, it's a personal love.

Bradbury: Yeah, and I'm learning all the time. And the things that I can take back to improve the whole world. The whole world has cities. Most of them don't have as many problems as we Americans do. My hometown, Waukegan, Illinois, is a disaster; the whole downtown section is falling apart. Because the city fathers don't know what a city is. They go in with the wrong reasons. If I became mayor tomorrow of a city, overnight, boy, I'd be in there planning, and changing, and building, and improving, and my motive would be to make the city. And that would give me a personal feeling of triumph, which is more than enough, instead of just pure power, which the average mayor wants: he wants to be mayor.

Couteau: When did you first become intrigued with cities?

Bradbury: When I was eight years old and saw the covers of the science-fiction magazines. They're all architectural. We love science fiction because it's architectural. All the big science-fiction films of the last twenty years are architectural. *2001*, when you see the rocket ship flying through the air, it's a city; it's a big city up there. And in *Close Encounters of the Third Kind*, when the mother ship descends, it's not a ship; it's a city. It's so beautiful. And when the aliens come out of the ship, you want to go back in with them and go away forever. And when one of the characters does, your heart goes with him.

So we love architecture; we love the romances of places. And Paris: identifiable objects; London, Rome … if you took the Eiffel Tower out of Paris and the Arc de Triomphe, half the city would be gone, because of the objects: the romance of objects. And I've written articles which have influenced the building of these malls at home. I wrote an article called "The Aesthetics of Lostness." We travel for romance, we travel for architecture, and we travel to be lost. There's nothing better than to walk around Paris and not know where in hell you are: "Gee, where is this … No, I'm lost." And you say, "Hey, that's good." And you're safe. Lost and safe. And you can't do that in New York City. Once upon a time, you could. There's hardly a place where you can do that. Someday, someday: if I have my say. If I have my influence. But while we're waiting for that, the mall is the temporary answer. It is a city away from the city, because the city doesn't know what it's doing.

Corporations know what to do. Because they have to know: they have to make a profit. Profit is a great motive. But cities don't have to make a profit. Governments don't have to make a profit, do they? If the experiment doesn't work, they say, "Oh, what the hell; let's tax people." But corporations: you've got to make sure you know what you're doing, because otherwise you're out of business.

Couteau: What would you see as the ideal formula in the creation of a city if we were to take these various elements: the corporation, the citizenry that is affected, and the local government? How would the formation of a city come about?

Bradbury: First of all, you tell the cities: "hands off." That's what Disney did.

Couteau: The local government, you mean.

Bradbury: Yeah, because they don't know what they're doing. They have no knowledge; they don't have the individual knowledge that a corporation should have. You pick the people from your environment who know a city block, who know the local parish, who know the local aesthetics, whatever it is.

Couteau: So who would pick them? Would the citizenry…

Bradbury: Disney; myself. If you were to give me a project tomorrow, let's say in …

Couteau: How about the people affected? Would they have any choice in the selection?

Bradbury: Yeah, they would have a choice of being excellent instead of having the city dead. If I could do something to help my downtown in Waukegan, which is … All the shops are closed, so the people who own the closed shops, you say, "How'd you like to open them again? Well, come on and sit in with us; have some input here. It's like: you didn't know what to do in the first place, and the city is dead; we have to start from scratch."

Couteau: So you would leave it in the hands of nonelected officials?

Bradbury: Yeah, elected officials don't know anything about cities and how to build them.

Couteau: But how are we to select who is going to make these decisions that will affect us?

Bradbury: Let the corporations get together. That's how they build most of these malls. And they turn out very well. And they're getting better all the time. Because more and more restaurants, more and more really fine shops of all kinds. And there's excellence …

Couteau: Let me give you a possible conflict here. What if the local citizenry is at odds with the planning of the local corporations?

Bradbury: Well, they've got to be part of it, of course; sure. But if they don't want it, then you don't build it. It's that simple.

Couteau: So you do see a partnership of some kind between the two.

Bradbury: Oh, yeah. But the main thing is to have the people who know how to do these things. I know several people who know how to build these things.

Couteau: In researching for this interview, I've noticed that commentators have often made note of your ambiguous, or at least changing, relationship with technology. The obligatory remark is that you chose to downplay its role in favor of literary stylistic innovations while everyone else was exploring it. And then, when other writers were catching up with your own stylistic concerns, you gained a certain faith in technology and even, for the first time, flew in an airplane, after many years of avoiding them. Is this an oversimplification, and do you care to comment on your current feelings regarding high-tech?

Bradbury: Well, you know, when you're twenty, it's easy to be negative. And we just came out of, we were going through World War II and coming out of it. And so, it was a negative time. And then the atom bomb came along, and I got married in those periods: 1946, '47, I was courting my wife. And there was that day which you didn't experience because you weren't born. But there was the time, in the middle of the summer of '46 or '47, when they were going to explode the first super-nuclear warhead, out in the islands. But the scientists weren't quite sure whether the earth wouldn't catch on fire. What if the earth caught on fire and the whole thing went up? Well, the night before, you know, I think everyone in the world thought about it, everyone that could hear about it on radio, because there was no TV in those days, and it was primitive: a few thousand sets in the United States. So, you become a philosopher that night, don't you? What if this is the last night of the world?

So, it didn't happen, thank God. But nevertheless, it was a negative time, and out of that I wrote a lot of things that went into the *Martian Chronicles*. Including "There Will Come Soft Rains": the house that lives on, after the people, and talks to itself. So, it's all part of a time, and my being very young, in my twenties.

And then, as time progressed, I learned more about those positive inventions that give us freedoms. The Xerox machine is the freedom to have your own printing press. I couldn't afford one. There weren't any such animals; they had mimeograph machines, but they were too expensive when I was nineteen. So a friend of mine gave me money to publish my own magazine, *Futuria Fantasia*, and it cost eighty dollars to put out each issue. But I was only making eight dollars a week, selling newspapers on a street corner. So you see, it was impossible. And most people didn't own mimeograph machines; they borrowed them. Or they'd do the things at work. But everything's changed now.

We have the Xerox machine, everywhere; el cheapo, you can put out your own magazine. And now, we have the Fax machine, which is another printing press. Not only can you send things, but you can print things in your own house. So the ability to acquire knowledge and to dispense it is a thousandfold.

Couteau: Was your faith in government shaken at that time? After all, those were elected officials ...

Bradbury: I think that, politically, the world is mad: always has been; probably always will be. It's a bunch of chickens everywhere. They're all chickens. Look at what's been going on with our budget problems in America the last few weeks. I know a few senators. Al Simpson of Wyoming I love: wonderful man. Terrific sense of humor. And very opinionated. But so many of them have no opinions.

Couteau: You do have mixed feelings about government, then.

Bradbury: Oh, God, yes. Oh, sure! There should be no tax raises; more money should go back to the people. Again, no one wants to talk about it, but, during the last eight years, we've got employment for nineteen million people, new jobs; no one wants to talk about it. I said, Wait a minute, that's good! You want them to go back on relief? Then your deficit goes up. No one has done any research on how much of the deficit's already been retired through interest. We're paying interest on this deficit, every year. How many hundreds of billions of dollars of interest have been paid, and don't they equal the principal? We could retire the whole thing tomorrow and forget it. There would be no profit–that is, the interest–but, in effect, it's semantics here. The principal has long since been retired. So we should get on to the next problem. And because of giving the money back to the people, which we did, with lower taxes, we've got all these jobs. We've got a new tax base; we're taking in more revenue now than ever before in the history of the country. No one talks about that. Every year now, we've got forty billion extra dollars beyond what the revenue used to be. Now, who's spending that? Where's it going? Has anyone researched that?

They don't talk about it on TV. It's there. And it's every year. Who's spending our money, and what is it being spent on? These people are irresponsible.

Frank Lloyd Wright Jr. was a friend of mine, years ago, and he was part of an endeavor I had to build rapid transit in L.A., which had been destroyed. It was all there, thirty years ago. We destroyed all of it; now, we've got to rebuild it. Well, it's impossible. And anyway, he gave me the rule which applies to politicians. Put one million dollars out on the table to build a building, and it will disappear. Now put two million dollars out for the same building; it'll be spent. If you're foolish enough to put two million out there, the architect will be: "Well, what the hell–gimme!" So, these people can't be trusted with money; they're drunk. And they think they can throw money at a problem. That isn't it.

The problem of education is: where do you apply the money? It's in the first grade. And it's in the kindergarten. And if we don't teach reading and writing, we lose the generation and we lose our civilization. It has nothing to do with money. It has to do with the will to teach. The will to care. And you can't buy that. And we should test all the teachers and fire half of them next year. Because if you let boys grow up to the age of ten and twelve and they can't read, they're bored silly. Then they begin with the dope, and they begin with the gangs. And if we could solve the problem of gangs and drugs tomorrow with education, it's got to start in kindergarten. And they've got to know how to read by the time they're out of first grade.

The administrators don't care. I have listened to people lecture on this, and I'm one of the few that says, "Fire the teachers." Test them and fire them. And then all the first and second grade students must be tested immediately. And if they can't read, then you intensify the effort with your money there. Because there's no use in having enriched programs up in the eighth grade if they can't read them! I mean, it's madness!

Couteau: Do your plans involve a political role of some type?

Bradbury: No, no. There's no power there, and you become one of those dummies. And they won't let you … if you're inside the political scheme, you can't do anything. You're not allowed to speak up.

Couteau: I agree with you.

Bradbury: Yeah. The good things in our country are

coming from the outside corporate effort. EPCOT is a permanent world's fair, which I always wanted to have when I was twelve. Because I saw the Chicago World's Fair, in 1933, and discovered they were going to tear it down in two years. Why tear down something so beautiful that is a centrifuge for the young, to whirl people into life, so that when they come out of a museum, or a world's fair, they want to live forever? That happened to me with the fiction that I read and the world's fairs that I saw.

And then, finally, I was invited to create the interior of the United States Pavilion at the New York World's Fair, in '64. Can you imagine how excited I was? Because I'm changing lives, and that's the thing. If you can build a good museum, if you can make a good film, if you can build a good world's fair, if you can build a good mall, you're changing the future. You're influencing people so that they'll get up in the morning and say, "Hey, it's worthwhile going to work." That's my function, and it should be the function of every science-fiction writer around. To offer hope. To name the problem and then offer the solution. And I do, all the time.

This interview was conducted in the fall of 1990. Excerpts were published in the November 1990 edition of the *Paris Voice* (Paris, France) and in the spring 1991 edition of *Quantum: Science Fiction & Fantasy Review* (Gaithersburg, Maryland). The complete interview was featured in *Conversations with Ray Bradbury*, ed. Steven L. Aggelis (Jackson, MS: University Press of Mississippi, 2004).

* Automotive production was a thriving industry in Russia and, later on, in the Soviet Union (1929-1991). An automobile with a petrol engine was manufactured in Russia as early as 1896. Three years later, a Russian inventor named Romanov invented an electric car, followed by a battery-powered bus. By the time the USSR was dissolved, the nation was producing over two million buses, trucks, and cars per year, ranking sixth in global

production.
* A reference to the actress Meryl Streep, who appeared in public service announcements warning of the dangers of apples that had been sprayed with carcinogenic chemicals.

The Biographer of Paul Bowles & Other American Expatriates Talks about Writing the Outsider's Story. An Interview with Christopher Sawyer-Lauçanno

Christopher Sawyer-Lauçanno's recent biography, Paul Bowles, An Invisible Spectator *(1989; Ecco, 1990), was the first in-depth study of the writer's life: one that will set the standard for all subsequent Bowles biographies.*

Sawyer-Lauçanno was educated at the University of California, Santa Barbara, and at Brandeis University. He currently lectures in MIT's Foreign Language and Literature departments. His translations from the Spanish, French, and ancient Mayan have appeared in numerous publications, including the City Lights edition of The Destruction of the Jaguar: Poems from the Books of Chilam Balam *(1987).*

While visiting Paris and researching his next book, American Writers in Paris *(Grove Weidenfeld, forthcoming), a "group biography" of expatriate writers in Paris from 1945-1960, he spoke about his encounter with Paul Bowles in Tangier and his progress in portraying the history of post-World War II American writers.*

This interview was conducted in Shakespeare and Company bookshop, with its splendid view overlooking the Seine and the Cathedral of Notre-Dame.

Couteau: How were you introduced to Bowles's writing, and what about it led to your fascination with him?

Sawyer-Lauçanno: I was in Tokyo and met an expatriate American writer and his wife, James and Nancy Sullivan, who were Paul Bowles fanatics. In 1980, the Sullivans, my wife Patricia Pruitt, and I formed a group that we dubbed

"The Victims of Literature," in which we shared our own and other people's writings. James gave me the *Collected Stories of Paul Bowles*. I was absolutely mesmerized by his control, by the horror, by the kind of dark-night-of-the-soul writing that he does so exquisitely: particularly, I think, in the stories. I'd never read anybody quite like Bowles.

Couteau: What was it about his approach to the "dark night of the soul" that led you to embark on this project?

Sawyer-Lauçanno: Part of what's so unnerving about reading Bowles is that he writes in this absolutely precise terminology. The language in Bowles is not obscure; it's not difficult. To me, it's like cut crystal: every word is exactly the right word. It's a very conventional writing style, yet with the most unconventional things happening. For example, there's "The Delicate Prey," written with a totally detached yet almost lyrical voice, about a camel that is massacred, and a young boy who ends up getting his penis cut off and stuck into his stomach and sodomized. It's all described in these rather dispassionate words. He never conjures up horror by using sensational language. I felt I was in the presence of a master craftsman. He's not a hallucinatory writer. Céline, for instance, is a hallucinatory writer of tremendous power who also has a very detached, almost ironic, wry style. Bowles is not like Céline, and yet I think they share a rather dark vision of mankind.

Couteau: Céline is almost more of a disillusioned Romantic, whereas Bowles is more of a photographer.

Sawyer-Lauçanno: Yes, I think that's a good point. What Céline does is: he really gets inside his characters, and you understand their motivation. Whereas Bowles's work almost always springs from *not* understanding his characters. Their motivations are usually as murky to the characters themselves as they are to the reader.

In terms of literary style, I think that came about because, early on, he was influenced by Gide and then by Sartre and Camus. He's been regarded as the first, and maybe the only, American existentialist. When the *New York Times Literary Review* reviewed *Invisible Spectator*, the headline read: "The Man who Discovered Alienation.'" I thought it was totally ludicrous, but, nonetheless, there is something to it. He was one of the first American writers to really zero in on man alienated from himself. Therefore, man retreats into a landscape. Where Bowles is really best is in dealing with man and landscape. *The Sheltering Sky* has four major characters: Port, Kit, Tunner, and the desert. He always says the desert is the protagonist of that novel: maybe the major protagonist. It's certainly the only one that comes out, in the end, as a winner.

Couteau: It seems as if it were his task to write about coming face-to-face with the *horror vacui*: about his relationship to a sense of emptiness in the cosmos rather than, as many writers choose to record, about human relationships.

Sawyer-Lauçanno: Yes, I think so. I don't know that he would say that. From what I know, at least, I don't think he ever planned it out that way or ever thought about it in those terms.

Couteau: Describe your initial meeting with Bowles. How did he react to your desire to write the biography?

Sawyer-Lauçanno: I wrote him what was essentially a fan letter. And almost by return mail, I received a letter from him, inviting me to Tangier.

I arrived in Tangier and, of course, I had no idea what to expect. I'd read these stories, and I thought he'd be living out in the middle of the Sahara and that he'd be totally menacing, dark, depraved, and depressed. In fact, he was this wonderfully charming elderly gentleman, impeccably dressed, with excellent manners, who laughed easily and enjoyed the company–or at least, seemed to–of those people who were in the house. It was something of a shock. I couldn't put it together with the man who'd written the books. Later on, I figured out what was going on, but, at the time, that was the initial impression.

I think when I got to know him better, I realized that it was a far more complex matter. He's very ambivalent about people. Those who think they're very close to him find out they aren't, inexplicably; and people who think he could care less about them discover that he cares deeply about them.

I think Bowles has practiced being the old gentleman in Tangier for a long time. Underneath that facade, though, is a person who's really rather nihilistic, like the work. I wouldn't by any means say death obsessed. But death aware. I don't know how often, after I'd say, "I'll see you tomorrow," he'd say, "Well, if I'm still here," or "*Inshallah*," which means, "God willing."

There's a definite morbidity. There's even, to some extent (and I think this comes from being detached a lot from New York or from his publishers or whatever), a certain irrationality connected with what he perceives as an exploitation of him by the publishers. It may be true. It may not be true. But he feels that, being in Tangier, he's always a victim. He's a victim of the Moroccans; he's a victim of the businessmen; he's a victim of the bankers, of his accountant, or of the IRS. Yet I think it's almost something that he enjoys. As opposed to being really upset by it, it gives him almost a sort of relationship with these far-flung institutions that he wouldn't have had normally.

When I returned to Boston, I became serious about the idea of a biography. When I wrote to him then, his initial reaction was, "I don't want a biography written in my lifetime." We continued to exchange letters over the next few months, and every letter would end, "Well, why don't you come to Tangier, and we can discuss it." So, I took the hint and revisited him.

I explained my intentions, but his response was, "I really don't want a biography written. A lot of people have come to me who want to do it. I realize that you're not out to defame me. But the truth of the matter is, I find my life really too painful, and I really don't want to relive it." He added that if I were willing to write a book without his active cooperation, then I could go ahead and do it, and he'd give me permission to quote from anything he'd ever written, published or unpublished: that I was free to talk to anybody I wanted to, but that he didn't want to have anything to do with the project.

All of that I found curious but also understandable. His autobiography has been criticized by certain people as being sanitized and not at all self-insightful. For instance, William Burroughs calls it "Without Telling." I think it was simply that there were certain incidents in his life that he would just as soon have forgotten.

On those terms, I felt I could go ahead and do the book. For the next six months I visited him every day, and, over a two-year period, I went back to Tangier three times. He was always willing to talk: to help me out with this or that.

If I asked a question he didn't want to answer, he'd just say, "I'm not going to answer that. We're not going to talk about that."

Couteau: It sounds like a peculiar agreement. He wasn't going to participate, yet he invited you there every day. I don't quite understand.

Sawyer-Lauçanno: I don't either. I have never quite understood it. His old friends tried to explain to me what it was all about. Part of it was that Bowles was absolutely interested in what I was going to do. At the same time he dreaded it, but he probably felt that it was better that I hung around and learned as much as I could, rather than have only a remote idea from those who have known him. Perhaps I had the best of both worlds, because I didn't write an authorized biography, yet I didn't write an unauthorized one either.

Couteau: How did the atmosphere impress itself upon your writing?

Sawyer-Lauçanno: I began to understand much more the *reality* of Bowles's writing. When you're in Morocco as an outsider, you're an outsider in a way that you are in very few countries. You're never sure what kind of footing you're really on. One of the things that Bowles does so chillingly is: he continually reminds the reader that, when you're an interloper in someone else's culture, there may be consequences. One is always aware of that in Morocco.

Drugs are very much a way of life in Tangier; it's a very natural thing. If you read Bowles, particularly his later stories, all of his characters are always smoking *kif*. This wasn't just Bowles's "take" on things; that's the way it is. One also senses the love Moroccans have for storytelling and the love they have for their own traditions, which are now dying quickly. Because of his translations, Bowles has helped to preserve that. In the old days, you went into a cafe and all the old men would sit around telling stories. Now you go in, and they're watching television.

Couteau: In every biography, the influence of childhood plays its part. In reading of Bowles's life, one is left with a sense that the emotionally brutal parental environment operates as an enduring specter throughout. Even the title of your book refers to this, in some way.

Sawyer-Lauçanno: His childhood *was* psychologically brutal. Like many artists, he retreated from the life he had at home–which was one of a totally repressive, almost maniacally despotic father–to the world of literature, and to drawing and to writing. And he invented his own universe by the time he was six.

There's a story of his called "The Frozen Fields." It's very autobiographical: about a young boy who has a brutal experience with his father. He has a fantasy where he believes that a wolf will come and devour his father. In a sense, I think that, for Bowles, writing was a way to devour his father. And yet the writing was a kind of salvation; it turned him inward.

He's very superstitious about evil, and he thinks that, by writing about it, he keeps it at bay. But I think that maybe it keeps the violent reactions that he would have had toward his father at bay. It keeps him from hating his father now. And he claims not to hate his father. But the writing is clearly about coming to terms with the fact that there's a certain amount of evil in the world, and it's irrational.

Who knows how these things work? I'm not a psychologist, but I would say that, obviously, there were some lessons learned in childhood that never really left him. One was that it was very hard to trust people. He learned, very early on, that he could trust himself and that, in a certain sense, he could create the sort of world he wanted, but that others who would come into that world may or may not appreciate it.

Before he moved to Tangier, he was thinking of coming to France. He felt that, in France, one didn't have to apologize for being an artist. This is something that he was keenly aware of in the United States: that an artist has no status in society. And yet, rather than coming to France, where there's some recognition of art or artists, he ended up going to Morocco, where there's almost no recognition of even Paul himself as a human being.

He took himself out of the entire arena so that he would always be able to live in a somewhat superficial way in relation to the Moroccan culture. He would never be part of the culture unless he converted to Islam. I think that appealed to him. The idea of being able to wear the mask, of being taken just as a kind of superficial Nazarene, was a perfectly good way for him to live.

Couteau: The other day we were discussing how, with certain writers such as Céline or Henry Miller, there's an unmistakable sense of musical rhythm and harmony. You recently wrote a piece about *The Sheltering Sky* viewed as an orchestral ensemble. To what degree, and in what manner, did the musician in Bowles affect the process of writing?

Sawyer-Lauçanno: Bowles's first career was as a composer. The first few decades of his life were basically devoted to music. He wrote quite a lot, particularly for Broadway plays. In the late 1930s and 1940s, he was known as the man to write the music. Because Bowles was acutely aware of literature, the music for the plays had a resonance that the music of a lot of other composers didn't have. For instance, there's his music for *The Glass Menagerie,* which is totally unobtrusive, yet it perfectly echoes the sensitivity that Williams constructed. He had an astounding ability to realize music that could reflect a text. He knows exactly how to extend a vowel; he knows exactly how to collapse a consonant. He understands diction.

Bowles's art songs are the best things that have ever been done by an American, with the possible exception of Samuel Barber and Ned Rorem. It comes from having that extraordinary understanding of language that can be transposed into musical terms. He was also extremely fond of found elements. In some of the Latin American pieces, he takes folk songs, marimba, pieces from Mexican *son,* which is a kind of dance, and turns these into exquisite pieces on the piano that sound like a whole marimba band–and it's just a piano. So, there was a sense of knowing how to translate one medium into another. The leap–going from music to writing–was paved by the work that he'd done as a composer.

As for his writing, you take any odd paragraph almost, and the first thing you're aware of is that this is writing written for the ear. There's a definite rhythm. He's incredibly aware of long sentences: long, multisyllabic words with, say, two or three very short words. Not necessarily nouns but adjectives. He's very spare with his adjectives. He rarely uses "remarkable" or "extraordinary"; he uses "blue," for instance.

Paul has acknowledged that he conceived of *The Sheltering Sky* as a symphonic structure with three separate movements. The first section could be marked allegro;

things are happening. And then, suddenly, you get to the middle section, where Port is dying. The action slows down to largo. You have a lot of counterpoints throughout. You have Port and Kit almost alternating as a counterpoint harmony; you have the desert as another outside player. All sorts of these things are going on in the novel. This wasn't necessarily something he was consciously doing; he told me this was the way he heard language.

Couteau: You're here in Paris, doing research for your book on expatriate writers in Paris from 1945 to 1960. Who are the major writers you'll be discussing?

Sawyer-Lauçanno: The book begins with the Liberation on August 25, 1944. The reason I chose the Liberation is that it really begins the new era. It also provided me with a vehicle to introduce a number of characters. Hemingway comes in at the Liberation. Gertrude Stein is here, at her country house at Belley. Irwin Shaw comes in, assigned to a signal unit. He's a great Francophile; he's in love with Paris for the first time, and he's as ecstatic with Paris as he is with Paris being liberated. He's supposed to be going around writing scripts, and, in fact, he's just going around with his mouth open, looking at the Arc de Triomphe or Notre-Dame. William Saroyan comes through, and he and Hemingway get into fisticuffs.

Couteau: Many of the other expatriates had been forced to leave and to return home during the war.

Sawyer-Lauçanno: That's right. The Lost Generation had pretty much gotten out. And you also have a lot of young people. Lawrence Ferlinghetti is a young naval officer who lands at Normandy, slightly after the invasion, and discovers Jacques Prévert in the process. A young sergeant named J. D. Salinger comes and hands

Hemingway a bunch of stories he's written, and Hemingway says, "Good going, kid; keep it up." And then they write each other in Germany, where Salinger is sent on. He sends Hemingway some more writing, and Hemingway responds to it. Later, that becomes *Nine Stories*. The exchange of letters between them is quite interesting. Apparently, Salinger had a mental breakdown in Germany. In fact, he was in a mental hospital.

So, it opens with that great panorama of Liberation and then moves forward, into what conditions were like in France.

Then you had Janet Flanner, who was part of the Lost Generation, coming back to France and reporting on the conditions. And Virgil Thomson returning. You still had some of the old generation; at the beginning, you get this mix. The old generation, particularly the ones who came back, were very eager to introduce the young Americans to the French.

You also had the great advent of the G.I. Bill. And so you get, for instance, Ferlinghetti coming over to study for his doctorate at the Sorbonne. Louis Simpson, Terry Southern, and Kenneth Koch are all studying at the Sorbonne at the same time, on the G.I. Bill. You have Richard Wright arriving, as an already celebrated artist, invited by Stein. He sets up housekeeping in Paris and stays until his death in 1960. You have James Baldwin, who had originally gotten a grant through Richard Wright's auspices; he comes to Paris to see Wright and to be in Paris. So you've got this incredible influx of very talented and mostly very young Americans, and a lot of them men, because of the G.I. Bill.

Then the *Paris Review* crowd arrives: Peter Matthiessen, William Styron, and George Plimpton. I'm also going to be dealing with John Ashbery and Harry Mathews.

What I'm interested in looking at in this book is a sort of panorama. How do you live in a city after it's been devastated by war? Because many of them were in that war: they were soldiers. How do a people recover from a war? How does a literature recover from a war? And what was important for them in Paris? Why Paris? There were many reasons they were in Paris, but they were different reasons from those that sent the Lost Generation over here.

It was a tremendously interesting time, because the writers who were here were as much interested in what was going on in France as in what was going on with each other. My impression of the Lost Generation was that they liked to talk to each other, but with the exception of, say, Pound, or with a few of the really multilingual members of the group, they weren't particularly interested in talking to the French or reading the French.

The end of the book is the "Beat Hotel." In 1957, Ginsberg went to a little, two-bit, fleabag hotel on rue Gît-le-Coeur, found it was cheap, had great rooms, and a great location, and told everybody to go live there. So, you had Burroughs finishing *Naked Lunch* there, and Gregory Corso, Harold Norse, Brion Gysin: a whole group of people hanging out in the Beat Hotel. And that, in itself, created a kind of movement.

I'm interested in dispelling certain notions about the Beat Hotel because, in fact, these were very disciplined artists, for all their craziness.

Couteau: Earlier, you were saying that there's a notion of Burroughs as a crazy, spaced out, junkie writer, and of

Ginsberg as a "yahoo from New Jersey," and you felt this needed to be rectified.

Sawyer-Lauçanno: I'm interested in dispelling this, because both of them are extremely well read and aware of tradition. Ginsberg is a poet with a tremendous amount of learning, and it shows. You don't write "Howl" without knowing tradition.

What was beautiful about the Beat Hotel was that you had these people sitting around, night after night, exchanging ideas: talking about what was happening. The real connection they shared was that they were attempting to write out of a different place and to create a new literature.

There was a definite indebtedness on the part of Burroughs to Céline. For Ginsberg and Burroughs, Céline is the great master. I don't know if this has ever been acknowledged in print, but, in conversations, Burroughs acknowledged this to me, and I intend to write about it.

In a way, *Naked Lunch* is a fantastic example of a shared endeavor. Burroughs wrote all of it–that I'm sure of–but if it hadn't been for people who kept reading pieces of it and encouraging him onward, it never would have seen the light of day. They were all very much involved in trying to create a supportive community here, and eager to learn what was going on; and I think that's something that hasn't come out much. You don't write *Naked Lunch* by being on junk all the time, out of control.

Couteau: You want to impress upon the reader that this was not a break with historical continuity; these were people who were aware of the history of ideas in their field, and they reinterpreted them.

Sawyer-Lauçanno: That's right, absolutely. I think, to some extent, *Naked Lunch* is in a Rousselian tradition of wordplay, of language, of one incredible image laid against another. It is also Lautréamont; it's Rimbaud; it's a whole generation of French poets of fifty years earlier. And Burroughs is aware of this. The great myth is that all these works just sprang out of these guys' heads.

Couteau: Had some of the confusion arisen because of the new personas that many of them, particularly Allen Ginsberg, adopted in the 1960s?

Sawyer-Lauçanno: There was an image that Allen wanted to project of being involved with experience, and it's true to the extent that he's a person who tries to live fully. But it you've ever looked at bad beat poetry, you can clearly see the difference between "letting it all spew forth" and what Ginsberg was doing. I mean, he knows his Blake; he knows his Whitman.

I don't think he attempted to erase the fact that he was a voracious reader. But there was a tendency in the Sixties, particularly among the drug culture, to pick up on Ginsberg's dropping acid, or smoking pot, or sexual liberation, or whatever, as being the real root into poetry. Perhaps, but it's also because he'd done his homework.

Couteau: And we, the readers, will take what we need from these writers.

Sawyer-Lauçanno: Yes. Everyone reads whatever one wants to read into a poem.

One of the beauties of poetry, and of literature in general, is that I can read certain works at different times in my life and learn something different from them. I remember reading "Howl" as a teenager and feeling it as this irresistibly evocative, nightmarish poem about the world I was living in. I read it in a really subjective way; l wasn't aware of all the stuff that was going on in there.

Reading "Howl" over the years, it's always a different poem for me. I'll always have that wonderful feeling I had when I was fourteen or fifteen. But now I also have such awareness of all the other things that went into that poem. And I don't think there's anything wrong with being a naive reader. That's one of the beauties of literature: that you can take from it all kinds of things.

This interview was conducted in the fall of 1990 and later published in *Bloomsbury Review*, March 1991 (Denver, CO).

BOOK REVIEWS

Carl Jung: Wounded Healer of the Soul, **by Claire Dunne. (New York: Parabola, 2000.)** *Jung, My Mother and I. The Analytic Diaries of Catherine Rush Cabot*, **by Jane Cabot Reid. (Einsiedeln: Daimon Verlag, 2001.)**

The nineteenth century hosted significant progress in rationalism and scientific research, yet by mid to late century there was a resurgence of things of a more occult or spiritual nature, such as Eastern religion, parapsychology, and Madame Blavatsky's theosophy. In seminars from the 1920s and '30s, Carl Jung (discoverer of the archetypes, the collective unconscious, and the synchronicity principle) observed that in order for such nonrational phenomena to be taken more seriously, it was necessary to establish a scientific manner of dealing with them. This could lead to institutional structures that would legitimize the study of the psyche or soul.

One of the leading psychologists of the time, Jung was ideally suited for such a task, in part because he believed that, besides a sexual instinct, there was a religious instinct: that psychic energy was, in essence, spiritual, and that we are driven by it to become whole and to strive for meaning. He called this mythopoetic quest the *individuation* process: one rooted in universal patterns yet unique in its expression.

Although he preferred to be remembered as a scientist rather than a Madame Blavatsky-type of figure, Jung's work was promulgated by the New Age movement of the 1950s, '60s, and '70s. While academia resisted Jungian-oriented research, his ideas continued to transform fields as diverse as humanistic psychology, anthropology, comparative religion, literature, painting, and art criticism.

By the late '80s and early '90s, his ideas gained a wider audience as a result of the Bill Moyers interviews with Joseph Campbell (later published as *The Power of Myth*; 1988) and publications such as Robert Bly's *Iron John* (1990) and Clarissa Estés's *Women Who Run with the Wolves* (1992). In each of these examples, the spiritual dimension of his work comes to the fore while the scientific dimension recedes to the background. Given this peculiar turn of events, a study of Jung that focuses on his spiritual aspect is especially suitable. This is also the case since too many previous biographies have served either as an "official" Jungian homage that neglects to explore his darker side or as a critical attack from authors who, at the outset, equate "spiritual" with "nonsense."

Bearing this in mind, Claire Dunne's *Carl Jung: Wounded Healer of the Soul* approaches his life in an innovative manner. She chronicles each developmental stage with a minimal amount of narrative, weaving it into longer passages from Jung's own writing: primarily, his letters and autobiography. These comprise his most intimate expressions.

Although it's more of a primer of Jungian thought than a biography (the narrative is so minimal that it simply links selections taken from Jung's publications), *Wounded Healer* contains a valuable collection of spiritual reflections. In addition, it's a physically beautiful book, with reproductions of cultural artifacts; works of fine art; photos of Jung's family, friends, and colleagues; and examples of his watercolors and sculptures.

Dunne includes a succinct treatment of two enduring taboo subjects: the accusation that Jung was anti-Semitic and a pro-Nazi sympathizer (in the 1930s, during the rise of National Socialism, he published an essay on the so-called difference between Jewish and Aryan psychology; more on this later); and an homage to his former patient, colleague, and lover, Toni Wolfe:

> Thirteen years younger than Jung, it was she who [...] introduced him to Eastern spirituality, helped free his intuition from the bonds of his intellect, and brought him back to everyday reality if he was losing himself.

Jung's brilliance was exemplified by his discovery of universal psychic factors that are contained within everyone (i.e., archetypes). But the need to understand what is "generally true" about cognition and behavior led him to make generalizations of a cruder, less insightful nature. He believed that, between the personal and the collective unconscious, other dimensions of psyche were determined by a cultural and racial past: that national qualities were not only imprinted on us by the environment but that they were also, in part, inherent. While the notion of a universal unconscious remains his most enduring contribution, behind this spiritually uplifting idea we find lurking a shadowy dimension that includes crass expressions of racial bigotry and bias.

A recently published document sheds additional light on such matters. Jane Reid's narrative of her mother's extended analysis with him, *Jung, My Mother, and I*, contains the most comprehensive–and most damaging–record of these shortcomings. For example, when speaking

To her mother, Katy Cabot, about a neurotic Jewish patient, Jung remarks:

> [The patient] thought his problem was only religious; he did not know it was racial. He had a British upbringing and had gone to an English university, and just never realized that Jews cannot have that kind of bringing-up. He also treated his sexuality in a way that a Jew cannot afford to treat it–by being promiscuous…. the Jews are especially devoted to the family because they are nomads and not connected to the soil in any way […] they have a complete lack of connection with Aryans, who are rooted to their country.

Therefore, just a few years after defending his published views on "Jewish psychology," Jung was continuing to voice such racist ideas privately, to patients and therapists-in-training. The same year he made this statement (1941), however, he was also referring to Hitler as "sinister" and "infected by the Unconscious." According to Jung, the "Germans were in league with the devil, and had a lust for power which is satanic."

While Jung was certainly no Nazi (this document offers conclusive proof of that, as do other remarks made in private seminars held in the 1930s; e.g., see his recently reissued lectures on Nietzsche's *Zarathustra*), he expressed many of the same prejudices that the Nazis–and many Europeans of this period–were prone to. Besides being a product of those racist times, he attempted to integrate racial and national prejudices into his psychological theories, thereby hoping to institutionalize and promote them, implicitly and explicitly, in his publications, seminars, and training programs.

Though many of his actions were clearly pro-Semite (e.g., he personally assisted in the resettlement of Jewish refugees who were escaping from the Holocaust),* too many of his ideas on ethnicity and race were clouded by such biases. "In America," he says, "there is a bit of everything: Negroes, Italians, etc. and a large contingent of Irish, not a distinguished tribe, but a wild tribe of Irishmen, with manners that are by no means English." Elsewhere, he calls the Irish "utterly irresponsible!" He believes that one must have a psychological defense against becoming too impressed by other nationalities–a kind of justifiable prejudice–otherwise one "goes under" and loses one's national identity and character. (He also used this expression in a racist context in many of his private seminars when referring to his trip to Africa.) On Swiss Catholics versus Protestants, he remarks: "the Protestant [community] ... has nicer people, is more orderly, whereas the Catholic one is more primitive and less orderly. In a Protestant country, people have better relations with one another. The 'Church' in Catholic countries takes the place of the 'relation to people.'"

About 200 pages after this passage, which is a verbatim account taken in shorthand by Katy during her analysis with Jung, narrator Jane Reid (Katy's daughter, who was given the analytical records by her mother shortly before she died) adds, in a narrative commentary: "Katy returned frequently to the subject of Catholicism with Jung.... *It was only from Jung that she could obtain an unbiased opinion.*" (My emphasis.) Evidently, daughter Jane, who is a Jungian analyst, is also untroubled by such bizarre notions. (This is an unsympathetic narrative on the daughter's side, however, who was more identified with her grandparent's puritanical severity and who resented her mother's unconventional, "flapper" lifestyle.)

Katy Cabot began her analysis with Jung in 1929, and it continued until 1958. The daughter of a naval lieutenant who was assigned to international ports, she was often left in the care of boarding schools and convents in Europe. After spending many of her formative years there, when she returned at age nineteen to Boston to live with her parents (1913), she experienced a severe culture shock. This seems to be the event that set the stage for the psychic conflicts that follow.

While the adult Katy feels that she had more freedom than the average child, it's obvious that her family exerted excessive control over her early life. They envisioned only one possible role for her: marriage to a "suitable" husband. She does find a man who is suitable as far as social standing is concerned, but in terms of being a soul mate he falls short. After they marry, she feels isolated and bored, living in the backwater of a cultural void named Charleston, West Virginia. When her daughter Jane contracts TB, Katy takes her to Italy to recuperate. Once Jane is better, Katy refuses to budge from Europe. After her husband's premature death, she no longer needs to pretend that she'll eventually return to America.

As a result of her parent's obsessive focus on socializing so that she can find a husband, Katy develops a taste for what Jung calls "superficiality" and "nonsense." Although overly identified with her extroverted, "social creature," the need to develop inner values presses upon her, and the unconscious reacts by "forcing her under," with a depression. (Jung was ahead of his time in realizing that depression served a positive function, forcing one to reexamine life in order to live in greater accord with the authentic self.) This leads her to Zurich and to Jung: possibly, the only spiritual center available to her at that time. In a classic example of the transference (in which we project unrealized aspects of the self upon the analyst), her analysis is centered on her perception of him as a religious figure. He becomes a touchstone to deeper psychic levels that she feels she cannot attain on her own.

Jung suffered a heart attack in 1944 and had what is now referred to as an out-of-the-body experience. Hoping to ameliorate her affliction, he shares what was revealed:

> If, before one dies, one can tell oneself: 'I have scrubbed that floor well and with the utmost sincerity,' then one can die! But if you say, 'I haven't scrubbed that floor in a decent way,' then you are in for it. *Everything drops off of you when you die, but those things which you have really accomplished don't drop off.* When you die, you are on a par with a scrubwoman, [therefore] it's of no importance whether you have done one book or ten books, *but have you done that which you had to do, as well as you could?* ... If you have, then it's in you!

Afterward, in a fitting counterpoint to the bad blood that exists between Katy and her daughter, Jung describes his unique concept of "kinship libido." He defines this as a need to "establish the original family relation on a spiritual level":

As the institution of marriage expanded from couplings within a tribe to those with neighboring tribes and, finally, to those with complete strangers, the need to reestablish an intimate "spiritual clan" is intensified. "We [moderns] have a neurosis because the endogamous libido is not satisfied." Therefore,

> the analyst becomes the maternal uncle [Katy calls Jung "Uncle"], and instinctively the spiritual clan is established on a spiritual level. The patient and analyst are also the *carriers of civilization* because [through the transference] they establish the big family of primitives in which all are relatives." "The Self is a collective idea, which the Hindus call 'conglomerate soul' ... built out of many souls as it were [...] *We are related to each other through the Self* ...

Jung encouraged his patients to sever unhealthy family ties and to befriend those who establish an authentic relationship with the Self. He envisioned a community that was unrestricted by social expectations and governed by values that were truly *Self*-reflective.

An invaluable account of his work (and, so far, the lengthiest record of an analysis with Jung), the diary chronicles this attempt to create a psychological "family." The self-appointed patriarch of the clan is portrayed as a genius who often stumbled because of shortsightedness; a bright intellectual and scholar who also thrived as a gardener, gourmet, and sensualist; and the promoter of a transpersonal consciousness who was ever the egoistic celebrity. The diary also captures the gemütliche Jung: at ease before a crackling fire, kindling a pipe of tobacco, and warming to an intimate exchange of thought and feeling.

This review was originally written in 2001 and later featured at tygersofwrath.com in 2006.
* "Jung's unpublished correspondence from 1934 onward contains many copies of official *Atteste*, notarized statements

submitted to the *Fremdenpolizei*, the Swiss government agency responsible for admitting foreigners to the country. In many, Jung guaranteed that if for any reason these persons were unable to support themselves, he would assume all financial responsibility. These *Atteste* were signed on behalf of persons who range from those totally unknown today to those well known in the Jungian community, among them the French theorist Roland Cahan, and Jung's old friend Jolande Jacobi. Jung treated many Jewish patients without charge once they managed to get into Switzerland, among them Aniela Jaffé, who later became his secretary and collaborator on his autobiography.

Letters abound similar to the one he wrote to Heinrich Zimmer on the eve of his immigration to the United States, telling him of persons he had contacted on Zimmer's behalf. And he wrote many more to persons in England and the United States, often ordering them to '*help this Jew*' (his emphasis)." Deirdre Bair, *Jung. A Biography* (NY: Little, Brown and Company, 2003), pp. 459-460.

According to Bair, when Allen Dulles entered Switzerland in November 1942 he was secretly working as an "advance man" for the U.S. Office of Strategic Services (OSS) in Switzerland. (Dulles would later head the CIA.) "For some time, Jung became Dulles's 'sort of senior advisor on a weekly, if not almost daily, basis.'" The following year, "Jung became 'Agent 488' in Dulles's reports to OSS offices in Washington and London, and 488's dispatches were considered fact and figured prominently in the agency's operational policies." Dulles said Jung "[understood] the characteristics of the sinister leaders of Nazi Germany and Fascist Italy. His judgment on these leaders and on their likely reactions to passing events was of real help to me in gauging the political situation. His deep antipathy to what Nazism and Fascism stood for was clearly evidenced in these conversations." In fact, Jung constructed the first in-depth psychological profiles of political enemies such as Hitler. "By 1945 [...] Jung's views on how best to get [German] civilians to accept defeat were being read by the Supreme Allied Commander, General Dwight D. Eisenhower. Jung's analysis of Nazi propaganda was that it tried 'to hollow out a moral hole with the hope of eventual collapse.'" Ibid., pp. 492-494.

Jung would have been horrified to learn of Dulles's leading role in helping high-ranking Nazis escape persecution in the Nuremberg trials so they could be utilized as intelligence assets (see Operation Paperclip). Through the CIA's Operation Sunrise, Dulles also arranged to secretly relocate 5,000 Gestapo and SS agents to South America.

The Continual Pilgrimage. American Writers in Paris, 1944-1960, by Christopher Sawyer-Lauçanno. (New York: Grove Press, 1992.)

Literary luminaries such as Hemingway, Joyce, and Stein often come to mind in a discussion of American expatriate writers in Paris. After the Liberation, however, sweeping changes transformed the literary scene in the City of Light. This postwar landscape, largely ignored until recently, is the subject of this group biography of American writers who felt compelled to journey here, in search of a crucible of transformation not obtainable in the United States. Richard Wright, James Baldwin, Lawrence Ferlinghetti, Chester Himes, Irwin Shaw, James Jones, Harry Mathews, John Ashbery, and William Burroughs and the Beats are the principal subjects of this study: a diverse group in terms of style, yet many of them sharing similar perceptions of France and an abiding appreciation for the manner in which life in Paris nourished their art.

Beyond individual differences of lifestyle and personal history (e.g., James Baldwin living in abject poverty and just barely surviving with the help of friends vs. James Jones's affluent Ile-St-Louis comforts), Paris provided each of these writers with a cultural context that they could never find in the U.S. Even a Frenchman who was uninterested in literary matters accepted that the role of a writer was a legitimate one to play in life: not one to be viewed with suspicion or derision, as was all too often the case in America. This lack of a need to constantly "explain oneself"–and, instead, to be granted a greater degree of respect for devoting oneself to the Muse–was enough to provide many expatriates with a sense of enfranchisement and to propel them to notable artistic achievement.

For Lawrence Ferlinghetti (whose thesis for the Sorbonne explored the city as a symbol in modern poetry), this extended to a deep love of Paris itself:

> Paris was not equated in the least with his two-room "cave" or his meager living allowance. Life in the capital was elsewhere. Paris was mythical and magical, the city of poets and painters, of intelligence, of beauty: it was a place that was allowing him the opportunity to create himself as an artist …

Other expatriates shared this love but, like many of the Lost Generation, kept their involvement with the French to a minimum. James Jones, author of *From Here to Eternity*, preferred to use this atmosphere of creative freedom to distance himself from the literary establishment at home and to engender a greater creativity within himself.

Sawyer-Lauçanno portrays the novelist Harry Mathews and the poet John Ashbery as two who "penetrated well beyond the surface culture, who engaged themselves fully in French language, literature, and life, and who transformed those lessons into a unique contribution that adds to American letters." The chapter devoted to them is perhaps the most intriguing one in the book, and it contains much new information on their artistic development. In particular, the author explores the liberating influence of Raymond Roussel, whose work helped to transform Ashbery's poetic style and Mathews's approach to prose. Roussel's wordplay and linguistic experiments had long influenced the surrealists; his *Impressions d'Afrique* was cited by Marcel Duchamp as the most important influence on his creative thinking. Roussel, writes Sawyer-Lauçanno, "opened up for Ashbery the latent possibilities lurking under the most common linguistic constructions, allowing him, in Michaux's words, *'la grande permission'* to experiment with language." Harry Mathews summed up the mysterious writer's influence by remarking: "Roussel was the man who allowed me to write fiction."

Continual Pilgrimage is a beautifully written and informative exploration of the (often inexplicable) effects that Paris exerts on those who journey here. As its title implies, this exploration is an enduring one:

> In the accounts of almost all of the writers profiled in this book, Paris was equated with artistic freedom, with the ability to experiment, to succeed, even to fail without feeling oneself to be a social deviant.

While many expatriate writers were never accepted by the largely insular French society (a complaint still heard among expatriates living in France today), they were at least left alone, in relative peace, to pursue their peculiar calling. In the words of Chester Himes (whose *A Rage in*

Harlem was first published in Paris as *La reine des pommes*): "It was not so much that France helped me, but that it let me live and empowered me to concentrate on my work."

Published in *lift*, 1993 (Somerville, MA) and in *Bloomsbury Review*, April 1993.

First Fictions:
New First Novels & Short Story Collections

Tea in the Harem, by Mehdi Charef, trans. Ed Emery. (London: Serpent's Tail, 1989.) *From Rockaway*, by Jill Eisenstadt. (New York: Vintage, 1988.) *Toni*, by Fiorella De Luca Calce. (Montreal: Guernica, 1990.)

Throughout the 1980s and now into the '90s, first novels have frequently emerged that explore the coming-of-age protagonist and the thinly disguised confession reset in novelistic form. There's nothing new about a first novel relying so heavily on lived experience, but what's noteworthy is the continuing message of pointlessness, personal greed, and rapaciousness. In the words of author Mehdi Charef, "outstanding players who bring crowds to their feet all learnt their art on pieces of wasteland, in the survival of the fittest and the most selfish." That he's discussing soccer players is very much beside the point; this novelistic aside represents the epithet of an entire generation.

Of the first novels from this period, the bleakest to come to my attention is Charef's *Tea in the Harem*. Originally published as *Le thé au harem d'Archi Ahmed* by Mercure de France in 1983, it was recently translated by Serpent's

Tail in the U.K. Charef is a skillful writer and, after being published at age thirty-one, he's become the well-deserving recipient of critical acclaim. (Until then, he worked in an engineering factory in the Paris suburbs.) It's not hard to see why. There's a jolting, rapid pace to his prose, which deftly portrays the horrific imagery of modern life.

The setting is a housing project in the Paris suburbs where Majid, the son of Algerian immigrants, feels trapped. He's surrounded by a foreign culture, limited by poverty, and lacking in enthusiasm regarding the few options that are available to him. From the very beginning, we are made aware that he feels

> caught between two cultures, two histories, colors of skin. He's neither black nor white. He has to invent his own roots, create his own reference points. For the moment, he's waiting … waiting … waiting … He doesn't want to have to think about it …

Majid's ennui is fueled by the ugliness of his surroundings and by the high-pitched tensions that exist between the tenants of the housing estate. Merciless fights between husbands and wives, between race-baiting Frenchmen and a new generation of Algerian French, and between the bitter roaming youth gangs and the frightened older generation, who attempt to defend themselves against this explosive, directionless energy–these are some of the daily conflicts witnessed by Majid.

Tea in the Harem is a book solidly planted in the world of the 1980s, with its collective awareness of a glaring division between the "haves" and "have-nots." Yet, unlike Tom Wolfe's over-celebrated *The Bonfire of the Vanities*, here the point of view is focused from deep within the

Center of poverty. In Charef's prose, nothing is contrived; nothing is incompletely imagined. It's a treatment reminiscent of Céline, especially because of his rhythmic language and the incessant message of despair that builds, staccato-like, around two characters who bang their heads against the wall of life. While they do occasionally partake of a Célinesque "uplifting pessimism" (in the sense that dark humor may be vivifying), more often than not they fail to be uplifted at all. Instead, they attempt to kill time through a series of numbing escapes into booze, drugs, sex, and petty theft. Thievery momentarily energizes them, and it finances, once again, the cycle of escape:

> And when you do what you like, you're saying that you deserve better than what you've got, and that you've the right to a better life. And what about emotions and feeling! No chance! The main thing is to fight the despair, find something to believe in, no matter what it takes.

The problem is, no one finds that "something" to believe in, especially here, in the housing estate:

> The children grow up as part of the cement and concrete. They grow up and they begin to take on the characteristics of concrete: they're dry and cold and hard, to all appearances indestructible–but they've got hidden cracks.

This also applies to many of those coming-of-age today, who confess, in growing numbers and with a lackluster matter-of-factness, to being stymied by the pointlessness of it all. If the 90s hasn't yet assumed a character of its own, it seems to have magnified many of the darker concerns of the previous decade. For while Majid and his ne'er-do-well companion, Pat, are stymied by a lack of "challenging opportunities for employment," there's a deeper malaise tugging beneath the plot of an entire generation. The culture clash of groups portrayed here reflects a larger cultural fragmentation in the world today, with its resulting loss of self.

While Majid listens to the Sex Pistols sing "God Save the Queen," Alex, of *From Rockaway* by Jill Eisenstadt, attends a college party in New England where she also listens to the Sex Pistols (and the Dead Kennedys, and the Fleshtones). She's the only one from her hometown gang who goes away to college. No one else among the working-class group has the money, initiative, or smarts. After her successful (yet somewhat absurd) passage into campus life in New Hampshire, she returns to the equally absurd concerns of her gang, with its limited options in the small, narrow-minded world of Rockaway Beach.

While certain characters in *Tea in the Harem* suffer a cultural longing–nostalgia for the "old ways" and for their now irretrievable symmetry–in Eisenstadt's novel there's nostalgia for childhood (which is symptomatic of the group's fear of adulthood). As with the adults in Majid's surroundings, there are no role models worthy of envy. With nothing to look forward to, Alex's friends gaze backward: to fleeting emotional states that are no longer accessible.

Published after Charef's work, Eisenstadt's first novel shares notable similarities with his tale. Like *Tea*, it possesses the tone of autobiographical fiction. A note about the author informs us that she was "born and raised in Far Rockaway" and educated at a New England college–just like her protagonist, Alex. Rather than being burnt out, the characters of each book are simply incapable of ignition. Again, it's not just a lack of money that stands in the way; it's something else: something barely definable, yet as solid and unyielding as a concrete wall. But no one seems capable of comprehending the obstacle or overcoming it.

Finally, in Fiorella De Luca Calce's *Toni*, elements emerge that signal a reconstruction of the self: a slow, deliberate regrouping of a battered yet undefeated spirit. Toni's alienation from her parents causes her to wander through the rain ("Must have been walking in the rain for an hour [...] Was too angry, too damn cold"), where she–like the kids in *Rockaway*–succumbs to youthful nostalgia. Reminiscence leads her to a rooftop (where once "the spunkier ones even found a hideout on one of the roofs") and to an old shack. Entering the beat-up structure, she stumbles into an unexpected adventure. Attacked because of mistaken identity, Toni is gradually nursed back to health by a group of runaways.

In addition to suffering similar wounds as the characters in *Tea* and *From Rockaway*, the figures in *Toni* have been abandoned by their families or have been offered no other choice but to run away because of abuse. They encounter the coldest of all worlds, and they do so from a position of greater poverty and vulnerability than the teenagers of Majid's graffiti-strewn cosmos. Some are underage; some are running from the law; others are victims of sexual abuse. Yet banded together, they manage to construct a family and a household of their own. It's not utopian by any means, but it works. It takes a while for her to believe it, but Toni finds a handful of friends who matter to her and on whom she can count. As a sense of physical and emotional security develops between them, they reawaken to the challenges of a life lived in a world almost stripped bare of meaning.

In many ways, these are the children of Nietzsche's "second innocence": living with a minimum of illusion, they are heroic because they have resumed the struggle. Yet, as a result of their wounding, they remain numb. Their emotional lives–if not yet crushed–are feeble things that need nourishment and care, as well as fortification to protect them from further assault. Many are hardened on the outside (like Charef's metaphor of concrete), yet they remain too soft inside: susceptible to rage, and prone to imitate the cold brutality that wounded them in the first place.

The significant thing about this first novel by De Luca Calce is that it intimates signs of change and contains characters that offer solutions. That they aren't yet able to "infuse a transfiguration and fullness into things and poetize about them until they reflect back [one's] fullness and joy in life" (Nietzsche) is more than forgivable. As the century reaches its close, such testimonials show that the individual emotional life has been truly threatened by impersonal social and collective forces, chilling the souls of an entire generation of youth. It remains to be seen whether confessional novels like *Toni* presage the kindling of a new spirit or if they merely reflect a final, sputtering, Last Hurrah of the soul.

Published in *Bloomsbury Review*, April / May 1991.

Not Missing a Beat: *Guilty of Everything. The Autobiography of Herbert Huncke.* Foreword by William S. Burroughs. (New York: Paragon House, 1990.)

One definition of literature has it as that which "entertains and instructs." Yet, there's another kind of literary endeavor that offers an instruction too crude and bleak to be considered entertaining, and it's into this category that the present confession falls. Written in a flat first-person style that sounds as if it was first tape-recorded and then transcribed and edited, Huncke relates a series of grim (and often banal) tales of survival. A runaway turned dope addict, dealer, and thief, he scammed his way through Times Square, always on the lookout for a cheap fix or a "drunken bum" to roll. He survives by writing fake morphine prescriptions and dealing to the local prostitutes. Or by stealing. Or by manipulating his friends, hoping to get something for nothing.

As with any chronicle that touches on the raw nerves of the human condition in such a way that we are shocked at how horrible, indeed, life and the living of it can be, this memoir leaves one with a feeling of profound unease. It is a feeling, for instance, that runs throughout the work of Hubert Selby Jr. Selby's pain, portrayed in a masterly style, rattles us and becomes our pain. We are buoyed neither by a happy ending nor by a literary justification of the human condition but, instead, by his artistry in transmitting such pain into art. Although Huncke's work is not the stuff of high literature (and it's unfair to Selby to draw such a comparison), the content (if not the style) of his memoir fascinates in similar ways and produces similar feelings of woe.

Although he was later propelled to notoriety by his involvement with (in his words) "the so-called Beats," Huncke's down-and-out lifestyle intrigued the far less beaten William Burroughs and Allen Ginsberg well before either of them had achieved recognition. Columbia-educated Ginsberg and financially comfortable Burroughs (according to Huncke, "He was a member of the Burroughs adding machine family, and the family in general had money") viewed Huncke as a "character" who was more streetwise than either of them, and, at various times, they offered him financial or emotional support. Huncke introduced Burroughs to shady characters and experiences ("I gave Burroughs his first shot"), and he was later portrayed in Burroughs's first book, *Junkie*.

Years later, fragments of Huncke's writings were assembled and published as *Huncke's Journal* and *The Evening Sun Turned Crimson*. Yet, throughout his life, he envisioned himself not as a writer but rather as someone who merely enjoyed an association with those who led creative lives. Therefore, his importance was mainly as a behind-the-scenes figure. Indeed, had he not been associated with the Beats, this book would never have been deemed important enough to publish.

If one can judge a life by such a narrative, Huncke's autobiography is composed of a nearly meaningless, aimless "drift." The portrait that emerges is one of a hustler gamboling from scene to scene, from girlfriend to girlfriend or from boyfriend to boyfriend, using others and allowing himself to be used, as well. Viewed as a kind of social-historical document, one could commend its honesty and its ability to further reveal a world normally inaccessible to outsiders. It also serves to deromanticize the Beat legend, illustrating some of the gloomier, unseemly sides of a group that was not always–as Kerouac coined it–"beatific."

Published in the *Paris Voice*, Feb. 1991.

The Demon and *The Room*, by Hubert Selby Jr. (London: Marion Boyars, 1989.)

Harry White, also known as "Harry the lover," is a bright young executive at the Lancet Corporation. His desire for the "promotions and the money, property and prestige" lead him to cautiously place his love life on hold, fearful that the bizarre intensity of his passions will interfere with his striving for success. At first, he limits himself to weekend assignations, but after a year of such "good behavior" he becomes increasingly distracted at work, and he feels "a tension building up in his body." Finally, Harry rushes through his lunch so that he can spend the remainder of the hour walking the streets, "unaware that he inevitably would stroll behind this broad or that one until it was time to go back to the office."

Soon, he finds it difficult to return on time. He's overcome by an impulse that he can neither understand nor control. His wandering leads to a number of encounters that are marked by such ferocity, cruelty, and deceit that they border on the inhuman. Only his boss's belief in Harry's business potential–expressed through a series of threats and incentives–serves to curb such dangerous behavior.

Much of *The Demon* reads like a Pavlovian odyssey in which a man is controlled through promises of rewards that appeal for a while but then are no longer enough: the demon of other instincts–darker, more passionate fruits–

breaks into consciousness and redirects it to a haunted (and often incomprehensible) terrain. It's not only an unbounded sexuality that threatens Harry with psychic dismemberment; he's also driven to attain a perfect (yet sterile) professional "success." Although his inability to achieve a more balanced state of emotional well-being continues to disturb him, ultimately he's drawn only by emotions of the lowest common denominator: narcissistic sexuality; the thrill of petty thievery; and, finally, the fantasy of taking a life.

Harry's pain is the pain of modern man:

> Harry's life continued to be a series of little compromises, and reevaluations of ethics and situations; of readjustments to life and then unwilling and agonizing acceptance of them that necessitated little lies, which, in turn, demanded more lies and readjustments and reevaluations. And it was not with the worlds ethics and morals that Harry was compromising, but with his own. That is what produced the conflict. That is what created the pain.

In every superbly constructed line of Selby's shockingly brilliant prose, a grisly irony informs us not only of hopelessness but of how, when things have become so hopeless, they must go even more wrong before they may be righted. Selby doesn't advocate brutality as much as portray it; he records the violence of contemporary life. Yet he seems to hint, too, at something within man that clamors for transcendence of our existential condition.

Perhaps that's hard to see in a "typical" Selby sentence, such as: "He could feel the sooty grayness crawl under his skin as he looked at the scummy walls and floor, and felt the gritty sheets as their foul stench reamed his nostrils."

Yet, the authorial presence that recognizes such ugliness (through the character of Harry) does so in such a pointed manner only when there's an implicit yearning for something beyond that gross, mundane realty. Perhaps, that's what's most shocking in Selby: his ability to inform the reader of a tender vision lurking beneath the prose, and this tenderness is the very thing proclaiming–in such harsh and brilliant tones–the abject condition of our world.

Indeed, the key to the book is found here, where Harry muses: "But the inner man knew that when you take something away that a life is dependent upon, you must replace it with something of value." That statement could easily apply to Harry's inability to creatively reimagine his life. Yet everything that might lead to a harmonious "life fully lived" has been aborted from the start. When Harry cannot find contentment in the lifestyle of the Lancet Corporation, his imagination leads him to cruel, vicious emotional entanglements. In the quote above, what was taken away was his desire to steal; the replacement was an appetite for murder.

Unable to commune with his demon, Harry is made one with it: "It was as if his voice was coming through a tunnel and there was a stone coldness in the sound of his voice." At the end of his ordeal, he feels only the "numbness and alienation that allowed him to do what he had to do ... That numbness ... Deadness."

While Harry is at least tossed back and forth between worlds, the nameless criminal in *The Room* sits alone in a remand cell, scheming and dreaming a continual fantasy of revenge and retribution. For nearly three-hundred pages, a man stews in his own bestial juices, and we are privy to his every affliction.

Here Selby portrays the most desolate and desperate of men: one whose inferiority is compensated by a series of brutal domination fantasies. Fabrications such as an ingenious self-defense in a courtroom–after which he's followed by reporters, is interviewed, and then testifies at a Congressional hearing (in which he plays a leading role)– are interspersed with harrowing scenes of childhood victimization, humiliation, and abuse. The tale unfolds with Selby's impeccable artistry of the obscene, using the most vulgar rhythms of argot with a musical sensitivity and empathic awareness of the downtrodden and forgotten in society.

The extreme fluctuation between states of inferiority and superiority is a major theme in this portrayal, and the author doesn't flinch from the use of any subject that can be utilized to drive home the point. Imagining himself as a sadistic trainer of dogs, the protagonist scrapes their paws clean with a wire brush, wondering "how long it would be before he could see a bit of bone thrusting itself through the mangled flesh." As a result of his obsession, the "animals screamed and yelled until, with constant and considerate lashings, they learned to howl and yelp with great canine artistry." He confronts his own tortured self and describes his misery and agony in similar detail:

> And for krists sake dont smile. Whatever you do dont smile. Then theyll really get bugged. Youll really bring them down. All for you. Theyll find out whats making you smile and yank it away from you.

While the trajectory of Harry White's plight is a broader one–rising to higher success; plummeting to more miserable depths–the protagonist of *The Room* is more pitiful, his pain and terror more human. Rather than succumbing to the numbness of a demonic possession, he's simply left to ponder the futility of life:

> And anyway, whats the use? Everything will fall apart eventually anyway. Everything always ends up nothing eventually. I cant win. I just cant seem to win. […]

> Really doesnt make any difference where I go or what I do. May just as well stay here, or anywhere. Its all the same. And always will be …

His prurient imaginings and lurid, sadistic dreams compensate for his browbeaten nature:

> Theres always somebody bugging you. They just wont leave you alone. No matter how simple things are theres always some sonofabitch complicating things and fucking with your life. Jesus, this fucking world stinks. People are nothing but a bunch of shits. A rotten bunch of shits. They always want to screw you. You go in to buy a pair of shoes and tell the guy what kind you want and the exact size and everything else and he sticks something on your foot and when you tell him it doesnt feel right he tells you its your size and it looks great on you and all that shit and by the time you get home your feet are blistered and all fucked up and you cant even kill the sonofabitch or shove the fucking shoes up his motherfucking ass.

Reading The Room is a compelling yet painful experience, requiring in the reader an ability to confront stark portrayals of the human condition.

Published in *Bloomsbury Review*, May / June 1990.

Rediscoveries II, ed. David Madden and Peggy Back.
(New York: Carroll & Graf, 1988.)

The precarious life of books is the theme of this collection of forty-nine essays on works of "neglected fiction," which are celebrated by writers who continue to be pleasantly haunted by their memory. Some call attention to books that remain almost completely unknown. Others proclaim minor works by authors better remembered for other efforts, such as Ann Petry's essay on Roy DeCarava and Langston Hughes's *The Sweet Flypaper of Life*. Still others examine historically notable writing that has slipped into obscurity, such as Arno Karlen's essay on Prosper Mérimée's *Carmen*, the novella of 1846 on which the world's most popular opera is based. Karlen offers a fascinating look at the difference between the intentions of the original work and how it was drastically altered in its final adaptation.

This is the second volume (the first *Rediscoveries* was published in 1971) of what one would hope to be a continuing contribution to the preservation (or resurrection) of our literary history. In the spunky words of the editors: "One of our purposes in this book is to pay critical attention to excellent writers whose names are not James, Faulkner, Joyce, but Garrett, Bolton, Baker, Powell, Thurman, Williams (both), Cassill, whose large body of work ... suffers neglect by scholars." Contributors to this volume include Vance Bourjaily, Rosellen Brown, Maxime Kumin, Thomas McGuane, Clarence Major, Ishmael Reed, Lynne Sharon Schwartz, and Gore Vidal.

Published in *Bloomsbury Review*, May / June 1990.

The Far Side of Madness, by John Weir Perry.
(Dallas, TX: Spring Publications, 1989.)

The terror of psychosis–and the terrifying treatments to which the "mental patient" is subjected–remains a source of bafflement to the outsider and a source of frustration to many practitioners in the mental health field. Although the literature is fraught with descriptions of symptoms, diagnoses, theories, and methods of treatment, few researchers address the patient as an equal. Rare, indeed, is the practitioner who has come to view psychosis as a strange sign of health: as an attempt to heal, or as a stage in a developmental process that transports the subject beyond "illness" or "normalcy" into a positive transformation of the self.

Such an exception is John Weir Perry. His *Far Side of Madness* remains a classic in the field for all these reasons. Working in the lonely tradition of Carl Jung and R. D. Laing, who each viewed psychosis as potentially purposive and telic in nature, Perry describes the goals–and the terrible dangers–that are typically encountered in the psychotic journey.

Perry's work in traditional psychiatric settings led him to conclude that those in the thrall of an acute psychotic episode are rarely listened to or met on the level of their visionary state of consciousness. Instead, every conceivable way to silence them–to ignore or disapprove of their nonrational language and experience–was called into play, thereby increasing their sense of isolation, alienation, and so-called madness. (Although this book was first published in 1974, things have not substantially changed in state mental hospitals or in community residence settings. To explore the strange imagery of psychosis with a client in a counseling session is viewed as "feeding into their delusional system," and it is discouraged by psychiatrists and social workers.)

Perry's work with those in acute stages of psychosis revealed that their pre-psychotic personalities were the true source of "sickness." Forced to live an emotionally impoverished life, the psyche had reacted by provoking a transformation in the form of a "compensating" psychosis, during which a drama in depth was enacted, forcing the initiate to undergo certain developmental processes.

Such experiences, which are accompanied by rich emotional imagery, offer amazing parallels to classical myths and to obscure rituals of antiquity:

> The individual finds himself living in a psychic modality quite different from his surroundings. He is immersed in a myth world ... His emotions no longer connect with ordinary things, but drop into concerns and titanic involvements with an entire inner world of myth and image.

Although the imagery is of a general, archetypal nature ("imagery that pertains to all men and all times"), it also symbolizes the key issues of the individual undergoing a crisis. Therefore, once lived through on this mythic plane, and once the process of withdrawal nears its end, the imagery must be linked to specific problems of daily life. Thus, the archetypal affect-images await a reconnection to their natural context: to the personal psychological complexes (which tend to be externally projected).

The notion of a "reorganization of the Self" is central to Perry's approach to the psychotic journey. Extreme damage to the self-image (usually, through a mother's withholding of love) was a typical problem in the cases he studied. The injury to the self-image is so severe that, during a crisis, psychic energy leaves the higher levels of consciousness and is attracted to the psychic depths, where an archetypal process of renewal commences. The goal is not only to restore self-esteem but also to engender a "capacity to love and be loved."

For this to occur, there must be a connecting link with another human being (and not necessarily a link with a "professional"): one that instills warmth and trust. This encourages a forward progression of the inner-imagery (reminiscent of Jung's statement that a schizophrenic is no longer schizophrenic when he feels understood by someone else). Therefore, at this stage, "analysis" seems secondary to basic human kindness. In place of an omniscient psychotherapist, Perry posits the autonomous psychic process as a crucial factor.

Perry searched for and finally discovered a regular pattern of imagery and ideation in the psychotic process. The negative self-image is typically compensated by an "overblown" archetypal one, the latter manifesting in imagery such as that of the hero, clown, saint, ghost, or sovereign leader. In addition, there's a sense of "participating in some form of drama or ritual performance." Most significantly, ten sets of motifs emerged: symbols of the center; death; return to beginnings; cosmic conflict; the threat of the opposite sex; apotheosis; sacred marriage; new birth; new society; and the quadratic world.

Following the Jungian school of thought (from which Perry emerged), comparative symbolism and cross-cultural studies were used to uncover a holistic context, in order to view the motifs from a broader perspective. Further research led to the discovery of the same sequence of images in archaic religions and in other cultural phenomena. Most remarkable to the author is that "the myth and ritual form that resembles it is the principal and central rite of the civilizations of remote antiquity, and parallels the image sequence step for step." That is, the "ceremonial pattern of sacral kingship," found in the ancient Near East, the Mediterranean, Europe, and the Far East, which involves an annual renewal of the cosmos during the New Year.

Perry devotes an entire chapter to the psychic significance of kingship, and he refers to its importance throughout this work. Indeed, the correspondence is striking. In New Year festivals, we find "a creation rite also emphasizing the center, the beginnings, death and renewal, the sacred combat and sacred marriage, and the other elements of the process." The divine rites of kingship represent a projection of "man's spiritual potential as an individual."

Once such functions were integrated in the collective psyche, the era of the sacred king gave way to a new era: one ushered in by "great prophets" and "founders of the great religions," and characterized by a revaluation of the individual and the Eros principle. Thus, kingship reflects an archetypal pattern of growth: one progressing through dismemberment, reconstitution, and the rebirth of the psyche, paralleling "outer" historical processes (which themselves were probably based on inner archetypal correlates), and culminating in the Eros principle (the return to love).

He places the advent of this era of exalting Eros at around "the middle of the first millennium B.C." and he refers to it as the "revolution of democratization." The prophets and mystics proceeding from that time–founders of culture and "heroes with a vision"–underwent eerie, turbulent psychic experiences. Afterward, they communicated a vision that reflected not only their own transformation but also that of the broader society. The genuine depth experience, however, is never supported by the collective when in its "acute" stage. As has been noted by Perry and by others before him, the prophets of old would have been locked up in psychiatric wards by today's practitioners of "health."

The point of Perry's inquiry, and of those in that lonely tradition I alluded to earlier (it might be called the Romantic tradition in psychology), is not to "diagnose" artists, prophets, and mystics–not to label or denigrate the highest human values and aspirations–but to reexamine such rich transformation processes and to value the cultural elements that enrich human life. Thus, "Rather than what is pathological in mysticism, we ask what is mystical in its intent in psychosis?" Perry concludes:

> The content of the depths reached in the ultimate ecstasies is on the one hand illumination that enlarges the understanding, and on the other, rapture that fills the heart with lovingness.

The schizophrenic's obsession with "social reform" is viewed as more than merely a "complaint against the faulty parental world." For Perry, the ideation of a "new society" is a legitimate psychic concern that affects us all: a collective problem seeking a collective solution, and one that especially manifests in psychotic and visionary states of consciousness. He asks:

> With our secular governments, and with our diminishing trust in any generally accepted higher moral or spiritual authority ... where do we find our real governance–one that involves us in depth? I consider this to be the modern problem that the archetypal psyche is wrestling with in order to produce a convincing new myth that will satisfy the need of the times.

Society's rebirth is dependent upon continual psychic upheaval: a renewal of the social archetype rooted in each individual psyche. It is there that we find the true matrix of history. And when social institutions become too rigid, it is there that we uncover a creative means of transforming them.

Published in *Bloomsbury Review*, March / April 1990.

Eros and Pathos: Shades of Love and Suffering, by Aldo Carotenuto, trans. Charles Nopar. (Toronto: Inner City Books, 1989.)

The author summarizes this work as a study of "love and hate," "pain, creativity, power," and "the need to balance outer life with the knowledge of our inner world." The guidelines are set along traditional Jungian notions: love becomes a catalyst, propelling an encounter with the unconscious. As such, it is intermingled with the shadow archetype and will constellate "negative elements as well." Because it involves archetypal energies, the polar opposite of love–hatred–is expected to emerge: "The conflict between love and hate is always present in passionate relationships even if it remains unconscious." The unique experience of love positions the lovers against the collective society by virtue of this uniqueness, and it challenges the lovers' notions of individual versus collective life. Yet there remains the danger of seeking, in the lover, "a lost wholeness." By projecting unrealized aspects of our psyche onto the beloved, we chase after our undeveloped self-image: "the beloved always symbolizes the potential of the lover."

While there is a single qualifier to this idea of love as a mere projection ("it is never a question of pure and simple projection ... We cannot say that love is 'nothing but' an illusion"), much of the remainder of the author's presentation is in the vein of the projection / re-collection formula of Jungian individuation: we project parts of our psyche and must re-collect them, and love is no exception.

Although this view has its merits, such a one-sided emphasis inevitably leads to a reductionist approach. After reading about "the image we carry within" in one Jungian study after another, the "inner image" tends to obliterate the image without–in this case, the loved one. The author's statement that "only through love can we really get to know ourselves" exemplifies this focus on the self and not the other: an unintended irony when one considers that the primary subject of this book is that of love.

When dealing with topics such as eros and pathos, one may unwittingly succumb to generalizations that lack the uniqueness the author so admires: "Love makes life intense and meaningful"; "We are what we are thanks to what we have been"; "The power drive can be truly diabolical" and

"Poets have no need to study psychology or psychoanalysis in order to express the profound truths of existence" are some examples. Perhaps as a way of acknowledging the ineffable nature of love and suffering, throughout the text the author includes poems by Dylan Thomas, Rainer Maria Rilke, John Donne, Walt Whitman, and others. Paul Klee's "Love Song by the New Moon" provides a fitting cover illustration, with its motifs of dismemberment and its heart-shaped hieroglyphs.

Of all the issues treated in *Eros and Pathos*, the psychic function of solitude is the one most clearly articulated: "In solitude we represent a truth that can unmask and denounce the falsity that circulates in the external world. The great figures of the world ... drew their truths from the wells of their solitude." Therefore, a person who upholds creativity as the highest value is the "natural enemy of power." As opposed to those who exist merely to dominate, "the creative act ... represents the possibility of living rather than simply surviving."

Carotenuto concludes with thoughts on how to confront fear and on the development of one's individual pattern as the reality that must be lived.

Published in *Bloomsbury Review*, March / April 1990.

The Homeless Mentally Ill. A Task Force Report of the American Psychiatric Association, ed. H. Richard Lamb, MD. (Arlington, VA: American Psychiatric Association, 1984.)

This task-force report of the American Psychiatric Association includes fourteen essays that contain recommendations for dealing with the mentally ill homeless. Among these are proposals for an increase in supervised community housing, psychiatric and rehabilitative services, medical care, and crisis service. Sensible goals, such as the availability of at least one provider for each "chronically mentally ill" person in need, are mixed with the unfortunate consensus of those involved with this report to "change the laws in order to facilitate involuntary treatment." Additional recommendations include combating a lack of coordination in the network of funding- and treatment agencies; increasing research and data-gathering analysis; and financing the development of long-term solutions.

Published in *Bloomsbury Review*, March / April 1990.

Schizophrenia: Treatment, Process and Outcome, by Thomas H. McGlashan and Christopher J. Keats. (Arlington, VA: American Psychiatric Press, 1989.)

Intrigued by the often mysterious causes of remission in the schizophrenic process, the authors of this study turned to an extensive archive of psychoanalytic case histories compiled at the Chestnut Lodge Hospital in Rockville, Maryland. Isolating cases with a particularly positive or negative treatment outcome and then reexamining them with a special focus on the interpersonal processes (particularly those between the patient and the doctor), the researchers hoped to proceed from individual case histories to arrive at a theory of what patterns are likely to emerge in a successful or unsuccessful treatment.

With this purpose in mind, four case histories are presented in a clear, accessible style. Subsequent chapters use narrative material to explore the characteristics of the schizophrenic experience. Finally, the authors describe a series of stages, including engagement, attachment, communication, fortification, and integration, each paralleling a stage in the patients' "relationship complexity," "maturation level," and "predicted long-term outcome."

Although the authors acknowledge a bias toward a medical and psychoanalytic orientation, a broader philosophical bias colors this study. For instance, one patient's interest in meditation, which appears to provide a positive, stabilizing influence, is termed "a narcissistic preoccupation." Similarly, the patient's discussion of poetry, reincarnation, and philosophy is characterized as "an effort to rationalize his difficulties." Other value judgments regarding the manner in which one adjusts to society and assumes various roles exemplify similar therapeutic biases.

While those working with a medical or psychoanalytic orientation may find this study of interest, one would hope that they would remain open-minded enough to meet the needs of the schizophrenic patient, who, above all, needs to be heard instead of being relentlessly judged and categorized.

Published in *Bloomsbury Review*, March / April 1990.

Alchemy in a Modern Woman. A Study in the Contrasexual Archetype, by Robert Grinnell. (Woodstock, CT: Spring Publications, 1989.)

The study of alchemical imagery and its parallels to the symbol-producing function of the psyche is a little known specialty in the world of Jungian psychology. Alchemists–the philosophically oriented predecessors of chemists–constructed elaborate images that strangely resemble the dreams and fantasies of modern patients of psychology. Taking a clue from Herbert Silberer (the Austrian psychoanalyst who first proposed a link between psychology and alchemy), in the last decades of his life Jung devoted a great deal of time to exploring the psychological meaning of alchemical research. He concluded that the alchemists had projected their psychic processes onto the unknown world of physical matter. Thus, they had uncovered not only chemical principles but important psychological principles, as well.

The latest Jungian to continue in this vein is Robert Grinnell. Focusing on the archetype of the internal masculine principle (or *animus*) in a modern woman, he uses alchemical imagery to explore stages of psychic development.

According to Grinnell, the modern woman is in danger of becoming possessed by this inner masculine function. For instance, by entering "as a rival into the masculine professional world," she is subjected to "strains and distortions," especially "in her diminished capacity to further psychological relationships." "In the 'modern woman's' psychology, this personal orientation has gone into partial eclipse." With her function of "relation building" endangered, she "is influenced by her unconscious masculinity in a way that is obvious to everyone but herself."

After enumerating the problems of the "modern woman," Grinnell introduces the reader to an analysand he calls "A." Hoping to use A's "case" as a paradigm of the modern woman, he explains: "her symptomatology centers on conflicts between her ego and her experience of the masculine component within herself." While he does go on to note a few specific symptoms, we're left largely in the dark about who she really is, how she feels about her suffering, or what she hopes to accomplish in analysis. For example, it's often unclear what her associations are to the symptoms and dreams that are discussed; whether she's even been asked for her associations; or if the author has already included them in his interpretation. It's nearly impossible to properly analyze a dream without a patient's associations–a point often made by Jung himself, which seems to be increasingly forgotten by many of his followers. Thus, the lack of personal detail about A results in distancing the reader, making it difficult to "feel into" her analysis.

This impersonal approach was intentional, as the author hoped to focus more on "collective" rather than "personal" aspects of the case. His interest is not only in therapy but also in the "deeper meaning of the phenomenon": one that "lies at the archetypal level." While this approach was successfully attempted by Jung in studies such as *Psychology and Alchemy*, here it just doesn't work. This is because he's not only omitted important details about A, but he's also failed to include relevant details about alchemy: the symbolism that might have helped us to explore a deeper meaning at the archetypal level. Instead, alchemical terms are bandied about without any credible link to the case, with the result that we're left in the dark not only about A but also about the relationship between psychology and alchemy.

Published in *Bloomsbury Review*, Sep. / Oct. 1989.

Encountering Mortality. *Full Measure. Modern Short Stories on Aging*, ed. Dorothy Sennett. (Saint Paul, MN: Graywolf Press, 1988.)

Old age is often thought of as an appropriate period in life in which to reminisce: to boil down experience into the quintessence of one's "story." While everyone's adventure is unique, common images emerge when contemplating mortality. In *Full Measure*, Dorothy Sennett has collected the work of twenty-three authors, most of them well known, who have attempted to portray an essential aspect of this theme.

A few of the pieces are noteworthy for their innovative plotting. In "The Dust of Yuri Serafimovitch," James Fetler explores the notion of self and soil. Yuri, an old Russian seaman and veterinarian, is offered shelter by the proprietor of a bookstore who refuses to purchase his unsalable old texts but who feels compelled to help him apply for naturalization so that he can qualify for a pension. Although the pension is Yuri's only logical option, he avoids studying for his naturalization test. Instead, he prefers to recall his adventures on the seas or to display his outdated knowledge of veterinary science. For him, reminiscence has become an obstacle to transformation, divorcing him from the present and therefore inviting disaster. He even clings stubbornly to a tin box that contains dirt from his native city of Murmansk.

Although Yuri refuses to prepare for the test, something about his sincerity convinces the government official to allow him to pass. As if acknowledging this destined transformation, Yuri goes to the zoo, "scattering the dust to the beasts ... Dust to the elephants, dust to the imprisoned cats. Like a planter the old man was sowing his dust." As if dismantling a tomb or scattering his own ashes, he pays homage to his past while accepting the challenge of the present.

In Joyce Carol Oates's "A Theory of Knowledge," the protagonist, Professor Weber, is secluded in a Gothic setting in the "foothills of the Chautauqua Mountains," with "freedom at last to compose his book on the foundations of human knowledge–freedom to sit in the sun for hours, brooding, dozing."

Oates's skillful portrayal of the intricate cerebrations of this crank nineteenth-century philosopher is an unexpected treat: "Nominalism would not triumph. The sleazy sordid Sophistic relativism of the Republic would not triumph over him … And it did not." His metaphysical contemplations are interlaced with biographical details, observations about the weather, conversations with his daughter (who looks after him), and sounds of the surrounding countryside.

While attempting to construct a unified philosophical system ("purify your thoughts … draw your ideas together before it is too late"), he's distracted by the occasional appearance of a strange looking young boy. Weber's daughter and the other locals ignore the obvious neglect and physical abuse of the boy by his parents, but when Weber hears his screams and discovers his plight he comes to the rescue. Although no one else is willing to "hear" the boy, Weber, feeling himself to be a victim of the philosophical deafness of others, whispers: "I hear you, I hear you" as he slowly shuffles through the moonlight to the child. As his philosophy is called into action, his normally distracted state of mind is suddenly transformed:

His mind, the consciousness with which he had been so familiar, had become wonderfully calm ... clear ... a liquid purity which he had never before experienced, as if another person or another aspect of his own being had taken over.

After he rescues him, the verbose professor simply remarks: "No need to speak! You're safe with me!" By putting aside his detached, intellectual approach, Weber emerges from his own entrapment and shares a rebirth with the boy: "They laughed quietly together, so that no one else could hear."

One of the most unusual characters in this collection is Conrad Aiken's "Mr. Arcularis," who, "in spite of ... his own dreadful certainty that he was going to die," miraculously leaves his hospital bed and embarks upon a pleasure cruise. Oddly enough, there's a corpse on board: perhaps, he wonders, a portent of disaster.

Once the great voyage is underway, Mr. Arcularis recognizes certain fixed rhythms: "people passing and repassing in their restless round of the ship." He notes "a kind of tyranny in this fixedness" and wonders at the "terrifying fixed curve of the infinite" and the "bright flash of death." He dreams of traveling through space: toward a faraway star. Finally, he befriends a fellow passenger, a Miss Dean, and he relates his dream.

A sympathy develops between them: one that blossoms into empathy and understanding. As their feelings deepen, so too does his sense of horror. For he continues to dream of "going round a star, the same terrible coldness and helplessness. That awful whistling curve ..." Once they realize that every dream is followed by his awakening in the vicinity of the coffin, they are overcome with terror.

Although they know he's moving toward his death, their

fear is eventually eclipsed by mutual love. Thus, when Mr. Arcularis enters his final dreaming, he is reconciled, and he experiences "not coffers, but light, delight, supreme white and brightness, whirling lightness above all–freezing–freezing–freezing …"

Aiken's ability to create a unique tale and to render this luminous, romantic setting gives the work a special feel, as does its ending: "At this point in the void the surgeon's last effort to save Mr. Arcularis's life had failed." Rather than the reader feeling deceived, this shift in perspective deepens the implications of the story.

One of the most powerful works in this collection is Raymond Carver's "After the Denim." As with many of Carver's stories, what sustains the reader's interest is his portrayal of ordinary people (with all their complexity) rather than the resolution of a superficial conflict introduced early on to maintain suspense. Carver's artistry is itself suspenseful: stunning in its precision, and painful to absorb as the emotional core of the tale is brought into focus. Often, he draws his characters along a line that culminates in a not-so-happy place. Here, an elderly man (whose wife is seriously ill) bitterly condemns youth for its carefree attitude; its unconsciousness of sickness, suffering, and death; its blindness to all that follows "after the denim and the earrings, after touching each other and cheating at games."

There are other works of merit in *Full Measure*, among them Bernard Malamud's "In Retirement," Stanley Ellin's "The Blessington Method," and V. S. Pritchett's "Tea with Mrs. Bittell." My only criticism concerns not the overall quality of the selections but the narrow cultural range they represent. For instance, only one story, by Arthenia J. Bates, contains African American characters: a mere seven out of 399 pages.

In her preface, editor Dorothy Sennett writes: "Selecting these stories and coming to terms with the necessary omissions ... have been less perilous tasks than one might suppose." That it was not experienced as perilous is unfortunate. A greater cultural sensitivity would have resulted in avoiding such ethnic exclusion and encouraged a greater variety of literature.

Published in *Bloomsbury Review*, March / April 1989.

Violence Against the Self. *The Betrayal of the Self. Fear of Autonomy in Men and Women*, by Arno Gruen, trans. Hunter and Hildegarde Hannum. (New York: Grove Press, 1988.)

Arno Gruen's thesis is that autonomy, which he defines as "that state of integration in which one lives in full harmony with one's feelings and needs," is often in direct conflict with the needs of society and with the collective rules that govern adjustment and the attainment of success. Indeed, our cultural history is largely composed of a "suppression of these feelings and the needs they awaken." The exclusion of such integral emotions leads to violence against the authentic self. As Gaetano Benedetti warns in his preface, "the roots of evil, of negativity, of psychopathology" may be traced, in part, to this blocking of one's essential nature.

According to Gruen, *abstraction* is one of the most destructive psychic forces, and it often leads to a fragmented personality. We "glorify abstract thought–at the expense of passion, enthusiasm, and openness," thereby avoiding a painful encounter with the self. The participation of science in abstraction's usurpation of core human values has only furthered this "split between intelligence and feeling" and led to a blind worship of rationalism. This, in turn, threatens the preservation of authenticity. Ironically, those who work hardest to maintain psychic authenticity are often "labeled as maladjusted and as failures." Among the so-called maladjusted are the prolific writer Henry Miller and the renowned mystic and philosopher Meister Eckhart, as well as many other artists and philosophers whom the author quotes at length.

Gruen provides an alternative to what often reads as an anatomy of the terrors that one encounters when turning within and facing the secret self. Although we may "develop a fear of fear itself," we need to:

> discover that though our fear is of complete helplessness–it is actually a helplessness pertaining to a specific situation. It does not have to be equated with total impotence and failure. Feeling helpless can instead lead to recognition of the limits of one's influence and the ability to accept interdependency.

A shift in mental focus away from an inflated, omnipotent ego and toward recognition of a "significant other" (through an experience of rapport, empathy, and open-mindedness) is a theme that runs throughout this work.

Certain specialists (as well as general readers) will view Gruen's reinterpretation of Oedipus as being rather provocative. He believes "Our betrayal of what we might have been, which lays the foundation of our destructive tendencies in general, is determined by our relationship with our mother." Yet he rejects what he calls the Oedipal "myth," arguing: "it is neither love nor sexuality … that makes a little boy in the Oedipal stage want to possess his mother. Rather, this is brought about by her often unconscious rejection of his authentic self." Thus, the child is motivated either to "serve her–or to dominate her." All this, he adds, "is not to blame her, for in this regard she serves only as a link to the father and to society, where the self is predicated upon power as the sole worthwhile reality."

Gruen is to be lauded for his sincere promulgation of feeling and of psychic authenticity (particularly in an age when psychology has had less to do with the study of the soul than with an obsessive, soulless accounting of extroverted patterns of behavior). Yet there are dangers in this approach, which rings of the literalness and one-sidedness that one often observes in a therapist's identification with the victim. For instance, it's necessary to separate the personal, literal mother from the "introjected" mother and from the "idealized" (or archetypal) mother. The need to establish a system of internal nurturing–of assuming the role of a mother to one's self–and the need to recognize and integrate the mother complex represent psychic realities that are not explored here. The naive or general reader is left only with a personal notion of "mother" and of "society," while a discussion of the mother complex and of the psychic determinants of society are also necessary if the authentic self is to be realized.

An honest approach to one's feelings involves an experience of nonrational phenomena, and if one is to "rescue" such emotions from psychiatric orthodoxy (as Gruen seems to be doing), then that rescue must entail an archetypal approach, as well. Instead, the author relies on a "logical" treatment that defends our need for self-expression through a method that is itself destructive because of its concreteness and literalism: its assigning of every problem to an outer causality located in society. But what is society? What is its psychic root? What do we project upon it? Statements such as "there are societies, such as the African Ituri ... or the Yequana in the Venezuelan jungle, where men are whole human beings. But in our society they are not" explain nothing and are, at the very least, questionable. The "noble savage" haunts this argument, as does an anything-goes "feminism" that charges all men as being guilty of numerous faults and that hails all women as being in possession of a multiplicity of heroic, endearing traits.

Tied to the Oedipal drama, Gruen tells us, "is the male conception of possession of power that comes into play."

> Men think of themselves in a logical, orderly way without realizing that it crushes their spontaneity, which they have grown to fear.

It's easy to grow tired of such generalizations about men and women, mothers and fathers, and individuals and societies, whether they appear in political discourse, in popular psychology, or in supercilious dinner table conversations. "Men are deeply tormented by doubts about their superiority," and "women who are true to themselves–that is, who are in touch with their own authentic life-forces–are never in favor of war." Therefore, what begins as a refreshing call to inner truth unravels in a welter of simplistic generalizations.

Had Gruen followed his own stated philosophy–of uncovering a voice that is unique to the self–then his goal of propelling the reader toward a genuine experience of inner authenticity would have been more convincingly accomplished. Thus, *Betrayal of the Self* is a summons to the creative spirit but not an example of it.

Published in *Bloomsbury Review*, March / April 1989.

Libra, by Don DeLillo. (New York: Viking, 1988.)

Don DeLillo's latest novel, *Libra*, is named after the astrological sign symbolizing balance and harmony. Here, the author of *End Zone* and *White Noise* has created "a work of the imagination" based on the life of Lee Harvey Oswald and the events surrounding President Kennedy's assassination. Libra was Oswald's sun sign, and, through the author's masterly treatment, it serves to symbolize a fictional Oswald's precarious search for balance in American society: a search that ends with a tilting of the scales toward excess and destruction.

In one sense, there's nothing new in the plot. DeLillo synthesizes elements of various conspiracy theories, including the involvement of the Mafia, anti-Castro forces, and a renegade CIA faction (each possessing a motivation and a means of killing the president). What's unique in DeLillo's treatment is the day-to-day interweaving of character, scene, and setting: the usual challenge of the novel, but here combined with an additional problem: believably reconstructing scenes involving well-known historical figures. Through the author's artful rendering of various stages of Oswald's life (e.g., a twelve-year-old Oswald talking with his mother; an adult Oswald stationed with his fellow Marines at a naval base in Japan), we come to believe in this fictionalized "Oswald" who desperately searches for his proper role in life. Conversely, DeLillo hardly fleshes out his portrait of Kennedy, correctly assuming that the reader's familiarity with him hardly necessitates it. Thus, JFK remains a larger-than-life figure who traverses a more distant point in the landscape.

We follow Oswald's odyssey as he serves in the brutal American military; works in a bleak Russian factory during a chilling winter; and interacts with shadowy CIA men. As he sinks to murkier depths, we also witness a troubling vision of America: one that includes an enormous clandestine intelligence network that spawned Oswald and that found a final place for him, as a patsy in the president's murder.

DeLillo's "imagined" Oswald doesn't always remain faithful to the historical Oswald; and since much remains unknown about the real figure, the author takes liberties with his rendering, relying upon poetic license. The imaginary "Oswald" possesses a smart-aleck smirk, a jaunty yet nervous bounce in his stride. He has much to offer the world, yet he lacks the education, the training, the right opportunity. He's a rolling stone bounding from place to place, all the while skittering to lower levels.

Finally our protagonist "defects" to the Soviet Union and works in a dreary factory where his potential for greatness remains undernourished. He tells the Russians what little he knows about the U-2 spy plane; afterward, pilot Francis Gary Powers is shot down, and Oswald is called in to identify him. He's uncertain if the man is actually Powers, but once Oswald has served his purpose he's shipped back to the factory. Disillusioned, he returns to the United States. The FBI nags him; his wife laments Mother Russia; his boss fires him for incompetence. Supposedly he attempts to enter Cuba via Mexico but is refused at the Cuban Embassy. Eventually he runs out of places to turn.

Oswald is portrayed as an antihero who effuses an air of inevitable tragedy. Besides being a victim of powerful secret forces, he also personifies a larger American flaw. Behind the exuberant persona of the Kennedys we encounter a backdoor plexus of power and corruption running throughout the land. It remains hidden from the populace until they're awoken with the crack of a gunshot, fired at the president. With Oswald we have the first visage emerging from this clandestine network and, upon seeing it, we're somewhat aghast: a young man in a T-shirt with a self-conscious sparkle in his eye, most remembered for a pouting grimace of despair just before his own assassination.

DeLillo follows the story through to the end, as a wave of despair ripples across the nation, and the mourning for one of most cherished presidents commences. The author succinctly reworks the historical material, creating characters who investigate Oswald such as Win Everett, Larry Parmenter, and T. J. Mackey: renegade CIA men involved in an intricate plot to kill the president.

> They wanted a name, a face, a bodily frame they might use to extend their fiction into the world. Everett had decided he wanted one figure to be slightly more visible than the others, a man the investigation might center on, someone who would be trailed and possibly apprehended. Three or four shooters would vanish completely, leaving scant traces ... then one other figure, one slightly clearer image, perhaps abandoned in his sniper's perch to find his own way out, to be trailed, found, possibly killed by the Secret Service, FBI or local police. Whatever protocol demands.

As in Plutarch's *Fall of the Roman Empire*, the fusing of history and imagination serves to generate a terrifying portrait.

Although he's only a minor character in *Libra*, CIA researcher Nicholas Branch emerges as one of the most intriguing figures. Serving as a counterpoint to all the "reimagining," Branch is so burdened with the assassination's cold, hard facts that his imagination is nearly short-circuited. He's sequestered in his "room of theories," writing a "secret history of the assassination" as he sorts through statistics, lists, diagrams, and the often pointless miscellany related to Kennedy's murder.

Indeed, Branch is besieged by a hefty supply of material from the Agency's invisible "Curator": a man he's never met, whom he doubts he ever will meet. He ponders a "roster of the dead": a long list of "people linked to Lee H. Oswald, people linked to Jack Ruby, all conveniently and suggestively dead." He admits: "There is endless suggestiveness." He meditates: "There is the language of the manner of death. Shot in back of head. Died of cut throat. Shot in police station."

The documentation proves to be too extensive to ponder long upon any one thing. "The FBI's papers on the assassination are here, 125,000 papers, no end of dread and woe." The Curator even sends him "Jack Ruby's mother's dental chart" and "detailed descriptions of the *dreams* of eyewitnesses following the assassination" as well as a "microphotograph of three strands of Lee H. Oswald's pubic hair." Branch symbolizes America's obsession with facts: facts lacking any trace of human relationship; facts that fail to reveal any deeper meaning; facts that need to be infused with creative imagination.

The transformation of fact into a wholly other creation is the "point" of all art, as well as its point of departure: its stepping-stone from the "real" into the transcendental. The reader's imagination is stirred by *Libra*; one is tempted to seek a balance as the scales tilt this way and that, propelling us beyond the merely historical and transporting us to a strange new terrain.

Published in *Arete: Forum For Thought*, March / April 1989 (San Diego, CA).

Love in the Time of Cholera, by Gabriel Garcia Marquez. (New York: Knopf, 1988.)

As its title implies, *Love in the Time of Cholera* is a creative amalgam of two starkly contrasting elements: the sacredness of love, and love's embodiment in everyday experience. Ultimately, the transcendental power of love emerges as the beautifully rendered theme of this evocative and paradoxical masterwork.

Throughout his oeuvre, Marquez has displayed courage in his willingness to explore a variegated stylistic repertoire. While *Love in the Time of Cholera* has formal similarities to his other great works–*One Hundred Years of Solitude* and *The Autumn of the Patriarch*–it avoids relying exclusively on the stunning, hallucinatory quality of the former or the lush density of the latter. Maintaining a folklore quality and grounded with the feel of everyday gossip, it incorporates images of love that hover between an otherworldly beauty and a netherworldly terror.

The historical setting of the novel is an "in-between" time: from the end of the nineteenth- to the first decades of the twentieth century. The location is an unnamed Caribbean seaport: one resembling Cartagena. Florentino

Ariza– who, with his long frock coat and melancholy air, resembles a "rabbi in disgrace"–is overwhelmed by his love for Fermina Daza, a comely girl whose "doe's gait" makes her "seem immune to gravity."

Florentino's antiquated attire and excessive sentimentality symbolize the romanticism of the last century, which is parodied and caricatured here and extended, like the frock, beyond manageable proportions. Indeed, he cannot even compose a business letter without incorporating lyrical flourishes. Love is his raison d'être, yet he reeks of it rather than shines, following always in its shadow, never seeming to grasp its essential light.

Florentino is placed in a precarious position when Fermina suddenly rejects him (after returning from an exile imposed by her father, who disapproves of Florentino for reasons of class). Her years of travel have so broadened her vision of the world that one quick glance at Florentino is enough to blot out every trace of her former passion and dreamy-eyed innocence. She simply tells him to "forget it," demands he return her letters and gifts, and promptly decides to forget he ever existed.

Fermina embarks upon "a marriage of convenience" to the esteemed Dr. Juvenal Urbino, who in many ways serves as a counterpoint to Florentino's overblown romanticism. After completing a "course of specialized studies in France," Urbino becomes "known in his county for the drastic new methods he used to ward off the last cholera epidemic suffered by the province." He founds the Medical Society and organizes the construction of the first aqueduct and the first sewer system. He serves as president of two academies and is conferred with honorary titles from various organizations. In one of the most powerful passages in the book, he and Fermina fly in the carriage of an "aerostatic balloon that on its inaugural flight carried a letter to San Juan de la Cienaga, long before anyone had thought of airmail as a rational possibility." Thus, he personifies a logical, pragmatic approach to life. Therefore it comes as no surprise that, when they marry, they do so in the absence of love. Even after they consummate their marriage, Urbino is "aware that he did not love her," yet he's "sure there would be no obstacle to their inventing true love"–like any other rational invention.

Love in the Time of Cholera is an "anatomy" of love. One of its most ingenious portrayals (in an anatomical and a visionary sense) is the growth of love out of the profane environs of "convenience." All the meaningless details of everyday life shared by two people bound together (all the unpleasant smells, degrading tasks, and dulling routines; all the unspoken bitterness and rancor; all the sullenness and gloom engendered by unlived possibilities) are unmercifully catalogued. Love's power to grow in such dark interstices–and to transcend life's profanity and to remain unscathed–is one of the more skillfully rendered themes of this work.

Just as love may transcend the limits of hyperrationalism, it may also transcend physical passion. Florentino's nostalgia is eventually transformed into an awareness of the reality of love as it must be lived, in the present. While Dr. Urbino's studies in France include his tutelage under the "most outstanding epidemiologist of his time," one "Professor Adrien Proust, father of the famous novelist," Florentino is fated to live in the haze of a Proustian nightmare: one that evokes a bloated nostalgia for Fermina at his every turn. While much of his time is spent traveling from one to the other of his 622 erotic assignations, through it all he still considers himself a virgin–untouched by anything other than his unrequited love for her.

After waiting half a century for Urbino to die, Florentino ends his self-imposed emotional exile (of fifty-one years, nine months, and four days) of unrequited love. He declares his "vow of eternal fidelity and everlasting love" to Fermina–while she's attending to her husband's funeral. Outraged by his poor timing, Fermina forbids him to return. Yet, through a series of letters that are meditative and philosophical rather than flowery and romantic, he persists. And then the final courtship of *Love in the Time of Cholera* commences.

Culminating in a steamboat voyage up the Magdalena River, the various themes of the novel coalesce into a symbolically complex and emotionally compelling adventure. Throughout this final chapter, Marquez deftly evokes the higher aspects of love while maintaining a dark earthy humor:

> he looked at her and saw her naked to her waist, just as
> he had imagined her. Her shoulders were wrinkled, her
> breasts sagged, her ribs were covered by a flabby skin
> as pale and cold as a frog's.

On the riverboat, Florentino considers a quote: "Love becomes greater and nobler in calamity." Later, as they paddle along and pass the sorrowful stretches of denuded forests, the "nauseating stench of corpses floating down the river," the "bogs of ashes," and the "vast silence of a ravaged land," the quote calls into question the survival of higher values in the midst of such decay.

Florentino's meditations also mark the inception of a new era: one that is as stripped of natural beauty as it is profaned in matters of the soul. Just as mankind was ravaged by the cholera plague, now the first signs of a humanly induced ecological devastation appear. Thus the voyage bears witness to certain historical developments. Along with personal signs of decay that reflect the aging process, we simultaneously witness the aging of Latin America and the world-at-large. The passengers are unnerved by such horrific images and are sadly haunted by all that is forever lost:

> the alligators ate the last butterfly and the maternal manatees were gone, the parrots, the monkeys, the villages were gone: everything was gone.

The imagery of finality is counterpointed by a human drama of "love eternal," comprising both the fanciful flight of uncaring youth and the inevitable conclusion of death.

Published in *Arete: Forum For Thought*, Dec. 1988.

The Mustache, by Emmanuel Carrère, trans. Lanie Goodman. (New York: Scribner's, 1988.)

A man soaks contentedly in a tub, toying with the idea of removing his mustache. Finally, he decides to surprise his wife, and he meticulously shaves his facial hair.

But Agnes doesn't seem to notice. She makes no mention of the change. He imagines she must be playing a practical joke and, trying to one up her, silently plays along. When they arrive at a dinner party, Serge and Veronique likewise make no mention of the missing mustache. He supposes she has forewarned them and has requested that they participate in the ruse, so he makes obscure allusions to his transformed appearance, even wittily evoking the image of Marcel Duchamp's mustachioed "Mona Lisa." His remarks, however, are met with indifference: no one acknowledges his "impeccably crafted joke."

After the party, his frustration increases once he's alone again with Agnes. But when he confronts her about the mustache, she denies he ever had one. When he displays some photos from their vacation in Java that clearly reveal him sporting a mustache, she impatiently asks, "What do you want to prove?"

The next day, when he arrives at work, no one mentions the mustache. Could Agnes have telephoned them? Even if she had, he doubts his colleagues would go along with such a hoax. And so, the question of his sanity is gradually raised: Is Agnes–or is he–crazy?

The elusive reality of the mustache is the first of many unsettling events in his life. When he tries to retrieve the photos from Java, Agnes informs him that they've never been to the island. She insists that Serge and Veronique never existed: instead of recently having dinner with the imagined couple, she assures him that they were at the movies, watching *Péril en la demeure* (Death in a French Garden). The gothic title is fitting:

> He already sensed that from this moment on, everything would accelerate, that any question he might ask, even if it wasn't a question, any remark referring to a shared past might cause his world to collapse even more. He would lose his friends, his job, his daily routine ...

When he asks Agnes about having lunch with his parents, she claims that his father's been dead for a year. In desperation, he drives to his parent's home, but he's shocked to discover that he can't find the house "where he had spent his entire childhood." He can't even remember the number of the building.

Convinced that "they were trying to drive him crazy, kill him, and he had nowhere to go," he escapes to Hong Kong. There, he spends his time riding a ferry dozens of times, monotonously shuttling back and forth between Hong Kong and Kowloon.

The setting, which resembles a suspended animation, is a fitting one, because now the question of perspective becomes paramount. It is symbolized by the boat's swivel seats, which passengers turn round to face whatever destination the boat moves toward. The ferry lacks a fixed stern or bow; instead, it possesses a "characteristic ... [of] total reversibility."

Here, the tone of the story shifts from a mystery to a work of alienation:

> he had to disappear. Not necessarily from the world, but at least from the world that was his own, the one he knew and that knew him, since the conditions of life in

that world were now undermined, corrupted under the influence of an incomprehensible monstrosity that one either refused to understand or confronted within the walls of an asylum.

The fusion of persona and core identity; the confusion of image with essence; and the contrast of playful imagination and painful reality: all this forms the texture of Carrère's *Mustache*. Its vividly constructed brutal ending serves as an allegory of the violence that confronts our time. It reflects the narcissism that fails to flower into a new wholeness and that–instead of bringing forth a value–devours itself, its transformative potential remaining unrealized.

This perspective represents just one possible interpretation of a disturbing creation that continually defies a fixed point of view and that invites the spectator to extend the book's horizon, through personal participation. .

Published in *Arete: Forum For Thought*, Aug. / Sep. 1988.

A Literate Passion: Letters of Anaïs Nin and Henry Miller, 1932-1953, ed. Gunther Stuhlmann. (New York: Harcourt Brace Jovanovich, 1987.)

Revered as a hero by his fans and disregarded as an egoistic scoundrel by his critics, Henry Miller lingers on in American literature as a presence for which no common consensus seems to exist. As with certain other artists who provoke a wide range of opinion, Miller symbolized a force or personified a notion extending beyond his own identity or creation. He belonged to a tradition in literature that was idea- or content oriented rather than one that was self-consciously poetic or merely well crafted. In style and in vision, Miller was unabashedly rapturous, entranced, ecstatic. Writing in the first person, he drew from personal experience to portray dramas that, when successful, addressed the larger issues of our time: mystical experience and the question of God; the contrast of the sacred and the profane and of meaning and meaninglessness (the latter quality often portrayed in scenes of exaggerated sexuality, for which he was later labeled a pornographer); the liberating role of the artist; the dehumanizing politics of the modern age; the spiritual value of marginal characters and of social misfits (many of them the "homeless" of his time); and meditations on the world-to-come. Miller was a philosopher in the original (and not in the modern) sense: one who *lives* his philosophy and whose philosophy emerges from the reality called life.

It's perhaps this philosophical view that stands at the center of a fierce difference of opinion on the author. To many "men of letters," Miller's worldview is unpalatable. Like fellow iconoclast Marcel Duchamp, he offended the traditionalists *and* the avant-garde (a nifty accomplishment) by refusing to accept a politically correct path, always preferring to go his own way.

Speaking of his own place in literature, Frank Harris (a client of the senior Miller's tailor shop) once wrote:

There are two main traditions of English writing: the one of perfect liberty, that of Chaucer and Shakespeare, completely outspoken, with a certain liking for lascivious details and witty smut, a man's speech; the other emasculated more and more by Puritanism and since the French Revolution, gelded to the tamest propriety; for that upheaval brought the illiterate middle class to power and insured the domination of girl readers. Under Victoria, English prose literally became half-childish, as in stories of "Little Mary," or at least provincial, as anyone may see

> the influence of Dickens, Thackeray and Reade in the who comes to consider world with the influence of Balzac, Flaubert and Zola.
>
> All my life I have rebelled against this old maid's canon of deportment, and my revolt has grown stronger with advancing years....

Although he epitomizes many other things as well, Miller clearly belongs to this tradition of "perfect liberty."

In contrast to Miller's liberation, Anaïs Nin pursued a style that approached the darker issues only to skirt about them with an abstract, denatured, Apollonian resolve. To integrate the "instincts" (as she liked to call them) into consciousness became a lifelong pursuit; one in which she was assisted by none other than Henry Miller.

In examining Miller's correspondence with his fellow writer, patron, and lover, we are privy to previously unpublished disclosures of intimacy and compassion that occasionally border on the electric. When the letters are somewhat less electric, however, they often fail to elicit the interest of the general reader or even that of the Miller- or Nin aficionado.

It's possible that the fault lies with editor Gunther Stuhlmann, who chose to exclude passages of general interest, such as (in his own words): "lengthy discussions of Dostoyevsky, Proust, Joyce, D.H. Lawrence; detailed critiques of one another's work in progress; ruminations on films, books, and so on, often encased in letters of twenty or more typed pages." Although one can understand the problem concerning the limitations of space, the decision to "eliminate material peripheral to the personal story" leaves the literary palate teased but unsatiated.

By focusing on the personal concerns and events of their

lives, the collection fails to pay tribute to the larger issues that propelled Miller to greatness and that profoundly concerned each author. Perhaps, there was a fear that Miller's superior grasp of such issues and his ability to more imaginatively respond to them would have severely overshadowed Nin's generally less interesting contributions. Heralded by the emerging Women's Movement and revered by a generation of introspective journal scribblers, her literary importance remains an inflated one, while Miller still awaits his proper canonization.

One hopes that such juicier ruminations on literature, film, and art will one day see the "light of print" and help to place each author in better perspective. Meanwhile, *A Literate Passion* occasionally sparks, but never quite ignites, the literary passions of the reader. .

Published in *Arete: Forum For Thought*, Aug. / Sep. 1988.

Mental Health Care and Social Policy, ed. Phil Brown. (New York: Routledge and Kegan Paul, 1986.)

The experience of reading through this anthology of eighteen articles on the history, changing social policies, and institutional structures of the mental health field is not unlike the experience of actually working in the present-day American mental health system. Some of the essays have the same distant, unfeeling touch of the bureaucratized mental health worker as they unfold into stretches of endless statistics penned with the peculiarly stunted tone of official reports. This is a format that has always seemed unforgivable to me when one is discussing psychological policy. Therefore, articles that discuss the same subject matters, even if the focus is on institutions and social matter and yet retain some sense of life are even more appreciated–just as one values the rare mental health advocate who's actually trying to do his job.

Not surprisingly, most of the essays that fall into the latter category are contained in the closing chapter: "Alternatives to traditional mental health services." Here we find an insightful study on the importance of "nonprofessional" client-run systems, by Audrey J. Gartner and Frank Reissman ("Those who help are helped most") as well as an article on the important (but poorly named) "Mental Patient's Association," by Judi Chamberlin ("The responsibility of the service is to the client, and not to the relatives, treatment institutions, or the government"). Anne M. Lovell and Yi-chuang Lu close the book with research that suggests the most interesting developments in mental health are not happening in America but overseas, in their respective studies: "From confinement to community: The radical transformation of an Italian mental hospital" and "The collective approach to psychiatric practice in the People's Republic of China."

Lovell tells how

> A man appeared to be hallucinating. He claimed to see dark insects. Rather than interpret the 'case' as might be likely in an American mental health practice, a group of workers accompanied the man to his house–which they found filled with little black insects. 'Treatment' thus became a collective effort to clean the man's house. Not surprisingly, his 'hallucinations' disappeared.

While Lovell concentrates on the transformation of a mental hospital as "but one chapter in an ongoing struggle against what was then defined as psychiatric oppression," Lu's focus is on the collective approach in Chinese society.

Lu reports on practices that American psychiatrists would consider heretical but that, nonetheless, far surpass our shallow "innovations":

> The involvement of the society is indicated by the practice whereby patients continue to receive their wages or salary during the period of hospitalization. Their jobs are held for their return.

The clients' peers are invited to the hospital to assist in their treatment and to provide support and "reliable reality-testing sources."

Unlike the American system, where an increase in client contact implies a decrease of professional status (with psychiatrists maintaining the least contact and highest status), Lu notes a "minimization of elitism in the interpersonal relationships in mental hospitals" and "observed a high degree of social interaction between patients and staff, and among patients themselves." Clients even conduct the equivalent of "grand rounds" upon each other:

> Each patient in [the] meeting reported to the group his own symptoms and problems. Then these symptoms and problems were commented on and analyzed by other patients in the group.
>
> At the beginning of the group meeting, I was surprised to hear patients casually using psychiatric terms and concepts. Later I learned [that] patients were given lectures on psychiatry. This process is called 'transmitting psychiatric knowledge to patients.'
>
> After the rest of the patients analyzed a patient's symptoms–the patient defended his own position vigorously–I was amazed at how easily the patients handled the criticisms of others.

The remainder of *Mental Health Care and Social Policy* (that is, the first three-quarters) suffers because the editors failed to select articles that transcend the predictable perimeters. Although authors were drawn from the fields of sociology, psychiatry, psychology, epidemiology, and social history, their general frame of reference is one of a hyperrational, orthodox sociological perspective (just as the orthodox perspective in psychiatry today is one-sidedly biochemical). Therefore, the book has the dangerous appearance of being modern and innovative while, in essence, it is not.

For example, we all know that the traditional American system is not working, is pitifully uncoordinated, is largely not client directed, and that it eclipses the client's cultural identity with a homogeneous mental health "culture." But a more significant problem is that the system ignores the inner spiritual life of the client, which leads only to further alienation. Unfortunately, the same approach is reflected in this collection. The notion of a "rational" social policy is implicitly woven throughout the articles, and this is presented as the panacea for dealing with all the woes of a failing system. Even the more interesting articles in the last section feature this view as a central theme.

If sociology is to offer anything of substance to the problem of mental health, it must make a contribution that extends unflinchingly into the complexities of inner life, thereby transforming the very fabric of the individual and, thus, of the group itself. Unless the sociological perspective metamorphoses into something else–something with an amplifying rather than a reductive quality–it can offer nothing to the individual separated from his inner life and from his outer society.

An exploration of such inner values and of their relationship to society would deepen the meaning of the social group and reconnect the therapeutically isolated individual to the collective. Yet, such problems are not dealt with here. Any mention of inner life is viewed as a threat to the concerns of the collective, instead of being recognized as the core matrix that is only secondarily reflected in the outer collective.

Inner life must not be ignored, or turned into some ultimate taboo, or looked upon as naive or "romantic." Instead, it must be met in its own right. Otherwise, the social perspective of societies of the past, which always pivoted on the spiritual center of the individual, will continue to be eclipsed by the "modern" policies described in this work, which advocate a rationalism that "rescues" the individual from a homogenized psychiatric culture merely so that he may be homogenized by the soulless policies of some spiritually neutered social group.

Published in The *Journal of Contemporary Psychotherapy*, autumn 1987 (Uniondale, NY).

Sense, Sensibility & the Solitary Child. *The Ultimate Stranger: The Autistic Child*, by Dr. Carl H. Delacato. (Novato, CA: Arena Press, 1984.)

In *The Ultimate Stranger*, Dr. Delacato posits the idea that autism is a type of brain damage affecting one of the sensory functions (sight, smell, touch, hearing, taste) and that *autisms*–those bizarre gestures that dominate the lives of autistic children–reflect various kinds of sensory damage.

For example, early in his research, Delacato observed a class composed of blind school children "waving their hands in front of their faces, tapping their eyes! I knew those behaviors were 'autisms,' but that couldn't be!" The director of the school informed him that the repetitive motions were referred to as *blindisms*. When he visited a school for the deaf, he saw children "hitting themselves on the ear. I heard strange rhythmic vocal noises. All in that same rhythm–the rhythm of the autisms!" To his great surprise, the director called the gestures *deafisms*. Delacato began to wonder if autistic children were actually brain injured. "Was the autistic children's alien behavior in reality their attempt to cure themselves? Were they trying to open up or normalize one or more of the five channels from the world to their brains?"

This fascinating first-person account represents a commonsense approach to autism. It also describes Delacato's unique treatment for autistic children, whose trials and successes are chronicled in detail. Just as he replaced the term *autisms* with the more suitable "sensoryisms," he also replaced outmoded treatment methods with a more humane approach. First he identifies the damaged sensory system, then he develops a treatment that allows the child to assist in managing his damaged function: "When I found which channel or channels into the brain were affected, I gave an outsized amount of stimulation to that channel."

For example, one child regularly bit her hand:

> Now it was clear. We took her hand, immersed it in ice water, then hot water, pinched it, even rubbed it with rough sandpaper and coarse towels. And the hand biting stopped! Nancy no longer needed to treat herself by trying to normalize the nerve channels between her hand and her brain. We did it for her, through stimulation, and her biting stopped.

He concludes:

> One or more of their intake channels (sight, sound, taste, smell, or feel) was deficient in some way. Their strange repetitive behavior was their attempt, through much repetitive stimulation, to normalize that channel or channels.

Delacato's typology includes fifteen sensoryisms. Each sensory function is categorized as *hypo*, *hyper*, or *white noise*. Children who demonstrated a hyperresponse "felt, smelled, tasted, heard, or saw too well." For example, those with hypersmell "vomit when they smell their own urine … many are so nauseated by these smells that they refuse to urinate or defecate until they can no longer restrain themselves."

Conversely, those suffering from a hyporesponse "didn't allow enough information to get to the brain. They needed greater stimulation to get through." Children with hypo-taste were "the garbage pails of our group, for they ... eat anything and everything. These children are dangerous to themselves, in that they will eat or drink materials that are extremely poor in taste, such as gasoline."

A third group, the white-noise children, suffered from extreme endosomatic sensitivity. They routinely experienced "internal sensory interference that decreased their sensory systems' ability to deal with the world." The auditory white-noise group heard "their own hearts beating, their digestion progressing, and their circulation, especially near their ears."

In a chapter titled "Reading the Sensoryisms," Delacato portrays the various groups. In "Treating for Survival," he explores treatments aimed at replacing the typical sensoryisms with experiences that transform self-destructive behavior and normalize "distorted sensory systems."

My only criticism of this work is the author's absolute rejection of the possibility of the psychogenesis of autism. In two chapters devoted to the subject, he discusses the pitfalls of psychoanalytic (read: Freudian) theory. But psychology did not begin with Freud, nor will the final word on the psyche be rendered by the adherents of Freud's outdated and reductionist theories. For example, Delacato's justifiable mockery of the psychoanalytic theory of breastfeeding, while informative, does not disprove the psychogenesis of autism. As a scientist, Delacato should recognize that the psyche is as complex as the physiological terrain that he explores. While it is true that the psyche cannot be reduced to the breast, it is also true that the psyche's influence cannot be discounted until more is known about this illness.

Delacato's sensory approach offers a promising alternative to those who suffer from this distressing illness. He's to be congratulated for his innovative work and for his decision to present these findings in an upbeat, lively style: one accessible to the layman as well as the professional.

Published in *Bloomsbury Review*, March 1986.

Reflections, by Henry Miller, ed. Twinka Thiebaud. (Santa Barbara, CA: Capra Press, 1981.)

With the publication of *Reflections*, the Henry Miller saga reaches a symbolic conclusion. No doubt there will be other posthumous collections of letters, notebooks, anecdotes, short stories etc. What is special about *Reflections*, however, is that here we have a chronicle of the "final moment": a work composed in the presence and aura of death.

Twinka Thiebaud, Miller's "live-in caretaker and cook," conceived of the idea to record from memory many of his dinner-table anecdotes. She writes:

> He offered criticism and corrections, and jokingly referred to me as his personal scribe recording his last words for posterity.

The most striking photo in the book is the one of Thiebaud and Miller joined in an embrace that exudes deep friendship and mutual respect. One feels that, finally, Miller had found a beneficent force–a female with no detectable trace of the femme fatale–who would become his friend, helper, and co-creator.

In her clear, concise introduction, Thiebaud says what needs to be said and then creates a portrait of Miller that is both provocative and amusing (particularly when exploring his "romances"). The brief chapters that follow are arranged by theme. The first is a dedication to his children that, at the very beginning, sounds the death knell:

I was lying in bed one day, thinking about my death ...

It's not only an unusual opening, but it's also a theme that we aren't accustomed to seeing in his work. Until now, the death theme in Miller's oeuvre has concerned itself primarily with "death in life": that is, psychic death and the need for rebirth. But now it's a concrete, biological death that he's confronted with.

This is followed by "Mother." Those familiar with his writing will glance at the title and recall the marvelous creations wrought of the bitterness and hatred he felt toward this monstrous figure. Here, however, in a manner more analytical than emotive or symbolic, new meaning is derived from the mother image that looms throughout his major work:

I wrote a short piece inspired by a dream I had a couple of years ago ... After writing that piece, my view of her softened. I had created a mother of my own making, one I could relate to, one I could love even. It occurred to me that if my mother had been like the mother I had dreamed about, perhaps I wouldn't have become a writer after all. I might have become a tailor like my father. I might have been an upstanding pillar of society like she wanted me to be. [...] Beginning with the earliest memories of my mother, I had saved up enough hatred, enough anger, to fill a hundred books.

In "Afterthoughts on June," we recall the hundreds of pages that were required to paint an enigmatic, elusive portrait of Miller's femme fatale, June. Yet, with this piece, he accomplishes this with a mere three pages of dialogue. As with "Mother" and many of the other chapters, one senses that he's finally been granted the ability to remove the veil of illusion and to regard his life pattern with a cool, Zenlike detachment. He's lived through, amplified, and recorded a monolithic personal mythos; now, in his final days, he can sit back and muse over what he's brought into being. Here he portrays June–perhaps for the first time–in a human light. June the archetypal *anima* and June the human being are now separated.

> After June and I parted ways that was it. It was as if she was dead for me personally. However, her memory was kept alive in the writing.

It is the grip of the archetype–as manifested through her–that has passed away. It will reappear elsewhere, in other women, but the vehicle of June will no longer suffice. The human aspect of June, which remains in the wake of the symbol, Miller calls "a wreck of a human being…. It was as if she'd been damaged to the core." He concludes:

> Our great love affair seems to me now like a self-created myth, a fairytale of sorts (though not always a pretty one). One day I was thinking about June and me, thinking, "Jesus, Henry, what was that all about? What in the world did you make such a big fuss over? …

The things that appeared at one time to be earth-shattering, even cataclysmic events, have now paled in the face of old age. They are dwarfed and stunted in the face of death.

This precarious balance between an emotional "self-created myth" and a more objective view–detached from the entanglements of the myth–forms the perimeters of *Reflections*. Apropos to this, Thiebaud writes:

Maintaining his illusions about a woman was far more important to Henry than learning the truth of her intentions ... He'd end attempts to enlighten him with statements like, "I'm not interested in the truth. I don't *want* the truth. I want illusion, lies, deceit. You could tell me she's a murderess, a liar, a thief, and I wouldn't give a damn."

This courting of illusion–of knowingly "not knowing"–has always been a fundamental aspect of Miller's life, art, and philosophy. From his earliest years, he was drawn to the mystery of life and of the self. He was gifted not only with a desire to explore such mysteries but also with a talent for articulating and re-creating them. Creative remembering and creative reimagining–essential elements of the mystic and the artist–were second nature to him. Yet, coexistent with this introspective, intuitive, heartfelt wisdom was a tough, acerbic, analytical self. At times, Miller would attribute this orderly, ruthless, pragmatic mind to his German ancestry via his mother who, though certainly no intellectual, possessed such qualities (or was possessed by them) in the extreme. In a chapter titled "My German Ancestry," he recalls:

> I was struggling to set myself free from their conventionality, punctuality, and super-cleanliness. I hated what seemed to be the most important part of my mother's existence–cleanliness and sterility.

Beyond these familial and ancestral challenges, Miller fought against similar attitudes in the broader society as well. There he saw the usurpation of feeling, intuition, and instinctual wisdom by the accepted norm of "rational" thinking and the rampant materialism to which it gave birth. Yet it was only by the strength of his own analytical faculties that he fulfilled his destiny and liberated himself from persons, objects, and experiences that would otherwise have paralyzed him with their mysterious allure, forming, as it were, the symbolic receptacles of his unconscious projections and fantasies. These congealed into a mirror of his soul, and it was this very process of gazing into the mirror of the world and re-collecting his soul–through the labor of creating of one of the most inspiring personal mythologies of our times–that would lead him to proclaim his love of illusion and brace him, with fearless resolve, to live out the calling of his desires.

Miller's philosophical proclamations did not always parallel his essential personality. It is less the feeling-toned mystic–immersed in the efflorescence of the symbol–and more the emotionally freed, insightful thinker that comes to the fore in *Reflections*. In part, this is because of the qualities of Miller the speaker, who was always more analytical than his poetic works might imply. But it is even more the result of this particular life stage. For all his praise of illusion, this is the memoir of a man intensely aware of the mystery *and* meaning that resides in the symbolic patterns of life. Here is the shaman contemplating his own skeleton, paying homage to the numinosity of the image while simultaneously examining the hieroglyphs that remain etched in the flesh. .

Published in *Nice* magazine, 1981 (New York).

Journalism

Allen Ginsberg's "Family" Album Exhibited

"Allen Ginsberg, Photographe." FNAC Montparnasse; Galeries Photos. 136, rue de Rennes, 75006 Paris. October 30-December 29, 1990.

Combating the rigid style of academic poetry and prose in the 1940s and '50s, Beat Generation writers, guided by the self-proclaimed "King of the Beats," Jack Kerouac, sought to render the "beatific" in life and art. Their work, though carefully grounded in literary tradition, stirred the consciousness of the day with a call to the spontaneous, provocative, personal, and lyrical yet vernacular use of language.

Critics of the Beats have disparaged the self-absorbed, narcissistic content in some of their writing. Although classics such as Kerouac's *On the Road*, Corso's "Gasoline," and Ginsberg's "Howl" have survived the brutal vituperations of academia, many lesser-known Beat creations have failed to transcend a focus at once idiosyncratic and egoistic.

Some of these concerns come to mind while viewing Allen Ginsberg's photography exposition at FNAC Montparnasse. Although Ginsberg was successful in transforming the personal elements of his life into a larger poetic vision, his attempts in the photographic realm often fail to hold the viewer's interest. While a few classic Beat images are included here (Kerouac posed heroically on Ginsberg's Manhattan fire escape; Corso and Burroughs visiting Paul Bowles in Tangiers), most of the photos remain of interest only to the most devout Beat aficionado.

These include a self-portrait of Ginsberg sitting nude and flabby in a yoga position, stoned and staring at his bathroom mirror (1985); several drab group portraits; and a photo of Ginsberg's former lover, Peter Orlovsky, visiting his family. The captions are handwritten by Ginsberg, and each tends to an overly detailed avuncular style, noting trivia such as the kitchen sink where Herbert Huncke used to shoot up, thereby immortalizing some rather obscure moments in "Beat History."

Although the exhibit suffers from self-indulgence, it also provides a few noteworthy glimpses of literary history. One photo of William Burroughs with a pained, lovelorn expression is striking in illuminating a little-known aspect of this innovative author; another captures an intensely self-assured Gregory Corso (the most primal Beat poet) radiating his unmistakable aura of survival. Other portraits include poet Anne Waldman in a tender embrace with Burroughs; the painter Larry Rivers at work in his studio; whirlwind Neil Cassidy–the frenetic spirit behind the Beat movement–uncharacteristically at rest in bed; and Lawrence Ferlinghetti (who published Ginsberg's "Howl") sitting alone in a San Francisco cafe.

Such "family snapshot"-style work exemplifies the theme of this year's Le Mois de la Photo, with its emphasis on avoiding the dramatic and spectacular and, instead, focusing on photography as a medium that expresses a more personal, intimate vision. .

Published in the *Paris Voice*, Dec. / Jan. 1990.

educates even those unfamiliar with the subject: "Selby once said: 'There is no light in my stories, so the reader is forced to turn to his own inner light' to make it through this journey. I now realize this is only partially true. The great beacon in his demonic oeuvre is that of the artfully crafted line and the immense vision of wholeness and transcendence that lurks behind it. Selby's empathy is there, omnipresent, even while recording the darkest hues of black. The utmost depravity is portrayed with the noblest verse."

After proving his prowess at the essay form, he turns to the heart of the collection: its interviews. These range from discussions with Albert Hoffman (activist and the discoverer of LSD) to interviews with literary figures such as historian and cultural commentator Robert Roper or poet Christopher Sawyer-Lauçanno.

One of the pleasures in this collection is that readers needn't have prior familiarity with the writers' works. Couteau provides that familiarity by the structure of his interview questions, which probe the foundation beliefs of each figure: "The first time I read your wonderful biography, I was struck by how supportive Cummings's father was. After all, he even paid Estlin to write *The Enormous Room*. And I was very thrown off by that. I always thought that artists are supposed to have a contentious relationship with their fathers!"

From the possibility that Nabokov suffered unconscious doubts about his own value that led him to insist that the world acknowledge him as a genius to the underlying patriotism of counterculture icons who were commonly seen as rebels ("Ginsberg continually affirmed that, essentially, Jack had always been a sort of patriotic American," says Sawyer-Lauçanno. "This had never not been part of who he was. It was patriotic to get into an automobile made in Detroit and drive across the country"), both essays and interviews are designed to make readers think about underlying psychology, social perceptions, and cultural change.

Readers seeking not just a literary presentation but a lively analysis of selected wordsmiths and their lives and influences must add *More Collected Couteau* to their reading lists. It's a powerful presentation that offers much insight and food for thought, and which should find its way into many a college classroom as well.
– Diane Donovan, *Midwest Book Review.*

Couteau's essays are informal, fervent, and well-versed examinations of the work or author at hand. At their best, they include fascinating insights into the significance of a writer like [Hubert] Selby.... The interviews are uniformly strong and include conversations with Michael Korda on T.E. Lawrence, Justin Kaplan on Walt Whitman, and Robert Roper on Vladimir Nabokov. Not all of them focus on literature: author Jeffrey Jackson covers the 1910 flood of Paris and why it's relatively forgotten, and Robert De Sena, in one of the best interviews, discusses his life as a gang member turned community activist. Couteau's passion and wealth of knowledge are obvious throughout the book ... and should appeal to many readers.
– *Publishers Weekly Select.*

Good luck trying to pin down Rob Couteau. Name the genre, and Couteau has almost certainly been there and done that. Poet, novelist, essayist, critic, journalist, memoirist, and travel writer, Couteau is not one to be hampered by constraints. He passes easily from one form of literature to another as if the borders between them did not exist for him. Perhaps they don't.

Couteau has been called a "literary enthusiast," and although he certainly is enthusiastic about literature (and indeed all art), the phrase carries the smack of the amateur about it, and Couteau is anything but. He is, in fact, an undeniably consummate professional. He is an independent scholar in every meaning of the word – unaligned with any institution except for the literary and artistic canon he so loves, and a thinker who comes to his own conclusions. [...]

This collection gives the reader a good sampling of Couteau's literary and scholarly talents, not the least of which are his interviews with writers he admires. Having spent many years as a journalist, I believe I have some ability to recognize and admire an artful interviewer, and Couteau is a master. His preparation is comprehensive, meticulous, and profound. His understanding of the process of writing in so many genres allows him insights into the particular problems faced by the writers he interviews. His style is conversational and relaxed, but deceptively so; he is always in control of the interview. This said, however, when a sudden fact or insight takes the interview down unexpected pathways, Couteau has the aesthetic nimbleness to recognize the opening and to follow it.

The collection features interviews with biographers, memoirists, historians, an inner-city antiviolence activist, and the creator of LSD. You'll also find herein Couteau's writings on literature, which I hesitate to call criticism since they lack the worst features of much literary criticism, which can be clogged with so much pretentiousness, cant, and philosophical obfuscation that it would take a plunger of Brobdingnagian proportions to restore a healthy flow. Couteau's essays are often rhapsodic appreciations and evocations of the work under study, and are stuffed

with both insights and joy. Consider this, from the essay on
Miller:

> And one of the great powers that surges forth from
> *Cancer* is the wit that explodes like a minefield beneath
> the reader when he least expects it. Again, at this stage
> of his career, since Miller had nothing to lose and only
> himself to please, he didn't give a rat's ass whether
> you'd be horrified, amused, or both. As is well known
> among the poor, humor is the one thing you cannot take
> away from a man who has been stripped of everything
> else. And humor is also the medium through which you
> will be reborn.

Couteau shares two things with Miller – love for Paris
and birth in another place that crops up often in this
collection, and which, as you would no doubt recognize,
the moment Couteau (or Miller, for that matter), opened his
mouth and spoke, as Brooklyn. Three of the pieces here are
about a trinity of writers beloved by Couteau and closely
associated with that famous borough – Walt Whitman,
Henry Miller, and Hubert Selby. It is perhaps that each of
these men shared in common an obsessive desire to
produce something new and revolutionary with their words,
something that was based not only on a powerful sense of
self but also on closely observed and unflinching
descriptions of their outer and the inner worlds in all their
ugliness and wonder. Lucky for us, Couteau is doing much
the same.

**– An award-winning journalist and a professor of
literature at Worcester Polytechnic Institute, James
Dempsey is the author of *The Tortured Life of Scofield*.**

Doctor Pluss, with an Afterword by Jim Feast

Rob Couteau describes *Doctor Pluss* as "fiction based on actual dialogues with schizophrenic patients, diabolically 'sane' psychotherapists, and well-meaning yet unerringly destructive social workers. It chronicles the descent of an eccentric, sardonic, and witty psychiatrist into what appears to be a state of complete madness."

His intention to metaphorically and realistically portray and contrast the madness of psychiatric process as well as its patients is powerfully wrought in a story about patients "surviving this holocaust of forgetfulness." During this process, their identities and personalities are lost in the institutional morass of a center purported to excel in rehabilitation, but which actually contains many ethical and personal challenges to the new psychiatric resident at the Walt Whitman Asylum for Adults, Dr. Pluss.

It's a place of rage and despair, of ambiguity where hope and horror run close together, and daily gives Dr. Pluss pause for thought about his patients and his role in their lives: "In her own unwitting way, Pluss mused, Evelyn personified the dual aspects of the godhead: horror and joy; awe and fascination."

Novellas typically are hard-hitting but often artificially succinct in their brevity. Often, one is left wanting for more. The best of them (of which *Doctor Pluss* is one) excels in taking this succinctness to its most logical conclusion, creating slices of life which are narrow enough to receive full-bodied flavor as the plot and characters develop.

One does not wish for more in *Doctor Pluss*. It's complete unto itself, exceptionally well developed, and emotionally compelling, connecting metaphorical traditional roles of doctor and patient, linking them in unexpected ways.

Each patient has their own special struggle with perceptions and illusions that influence reality. Rob Couteau's descriptions are often long and detailed, demanding a slower, more contemplative reading style than is usual in novels in general and novellas in particular. These long sentences are packed with description that grabs heart and mind:

> It was tragically convenient to blame her uncontrollable obesity and fierce primal appetite upon this crazy cat of the fleshy sphinx, this lazy Egyptian feline entombed within, lost in a drifting, timeless time of metempsychosis and crocodile gods, of the loopy eye of the *ankh* – a cross with a teardrop on top – mystic symbol for who knows what. Into the loop one entered and never again returned, adrift with the sacred crocodiles and lost in a thick bed of reeds asway in a warm, mosquito breeze, the muddy Nile lapping you along to your mother's teat which is the grand fan of the delta: lush black earth of Moses and Nefertiti and Alexander and Akhenaton, all had wet themselves in her deltoid lap – let me wash you clean with my dirty waters and raise your material soul to a vast glittering realm of *death, death, death* – great Egyptian fantasy that delivered us to Hades, where we left this paltry life of the living and gladly marched to the everlasting realm of the deceased.

Run-on sentence, or beautiful metaphor for a mental condition? Couteau is not afraid to push the literary boundaries of convention in pursuit of a different form of descriptive truth, bringing readers along in a rollicking ride through schizophrenic experience that ultimately questions the foundations of reality and perception from both sides of the therapist's couch.

His interpretations and descriptions of the schizophrenic experience are particularly astute, astonishing, and evocatively described.

When Pluss vanishes, a ripple of effects on doctors and patients alike threatens to change everything. A regression process takes place that questions both convention and traditional roles.

Readers who choose *Doctor Pluss* are in for a treat. It's like *One Flew Over the Cuckoo's Nest* on steroids: a thought-provoking examination of sanity, insanity, and the crossover process that leaves readers thinking long after this therapeutic slice of life is consumed.

– Diane Donovan, *Midwest Book Review.*

Reading *Doctor Pluss*, Rob Couteau's intense, dramatic story of a psychologist who works at the Walt Whitman Asylum for Adults, one might think, especially since there is no authorial information given on the book, that Couteau is a psychiatrist of some sort. How else could he write with such assurance about this milieu?

However, turning to his book of essays, poems, reviews, and interviews, *Collected Couteau*, though it, too, contains no authorial information, one begins to see that he is a well-informed layman who has thought deeply about psychological issues. Not only has he thought, but he has also forged a coherent philosophy through both the direct study of the subject and a close reading of literature.

Part of his philosophy is revealed in the interpretation of schizophrenia in a review of a book by John Perry. He notes that "Perry's work in traditional psychiatric settings led him to conclude that those in the thrall of an acute psychotic episode are rarely listened to or met on the level of their visionary state of consciousness." If care providers paid heed to what the patients were trying to show in their symptoms and musings, they would often find that, "forced to live an emotionally impoverished life, the psyche had reacted by provoking a transformation in the form of a 'compensating' psychosis, during which a drama in depth was enacted, forcing the initiate to undergo certain developmental processes."

Couteau quotes Perry concerning this state: "The individual [patient] finds himself living in a psychic modality quite different from his surroundings. He is immersed in a myth world." This modality may seem to be regressive, but it is far from unfruitful. "Although the [myth] imagery is of a general, archetypal nature," writes Couteau, "it also symbolizes the key issues of the individual undergoing the crisis. Therefore, once lived through on this mythic plane, and once the process of withdrawal nears its end, the images must be linked to specific problems of daily life." This leads, in the best cases, to a healing whereby the patient is now able to face and cope with problems that caused the flight into illness.

Perry's work is not that well known, but readers may be more familiar with the once celebrated theories of R. D. Laing. While not finding archetypes in his patients' thoughts, Laing agreed with Perry in treating the schizophrenics' attempts to communicate as valid efforts to reach out, and in finding that their psychological difficulties were often rooted in their untenable lives.

This is not to say that Couteau wholeheartedly endorses these ideas of Perry's. That's not the point. Rather, Dr. Pluss, the staff psychiatrist in the novel named after him, does. Instead of coldly and clinically assessing his schizophrenic patients (as dominant psychiatric norms dictate he should), Pluss befriends them, sharing his own passions, such as his love of modernist art, particularly of Paul Klee, in a workshop where the inmates learn to appreciate art as a form of therapy. Further, he listens carefully to them as they exhaustively recount their life views. He may criticize these patients' sometimes outrageous ideas, but he takes them seriously.

The description on the back of the novel states that the book is "based on actual dialogues with schizophrenic patients," something evident from the stories told to Pluss. With a fantasy akin to Freud's famous Rat Man case, one woman thinks a ravenous cat lives in her midsection. That's why she constantly has to eat. Otherwise, the beast, in its craving for food, will begin consuming her internal organs. (In Freud's story, the patient imagines rats gnawing on his friends' buttocks.)

The most significant patient is Jonah, who believes his own mental problems are so tremendously fascinating that, when he engages in a self-analysis (talking to himself), somehow the Viennese master himself comes back to life to eavesdrop. As Jonah tells Dr. Pluss, "And Freud listened to the analysis, glued to his television. He wouldn't eat; he wouldn't sleep; he wouldn't anything." Ironically enough, Jonah's psychoanalysis simply consists of enumerating, without explaining, his own situation. "I'm a patient; this is a hospital. Why am I in a cage?" While this fantasy may not seem terrifically engaging, when not raving Jonah presents thoughtful and provocative comments on religion, other patients, and even on Dr. Pluss, who is himself undergoing a nervous breakdown.

Pluss had been a painter but gave up the arts to devote himself to helping people. Now, as he is increasingly enthralled by some of his patients' mythic visions, he begins painting again. Using notes of his talks with schizophrenics, he recasts their ideas as art. He creates, for instance, a series of paintings on Jonah, who sometimes thinks of his mind as a clockwork. Pluss depicts "Jonah being cured of paranoia at the Bulova Watch Repair School and leaving behind his persecution complex in the grim milieu of the Bulova assembly line."

Couteau has some misgivings about the sympathetic-ear approach of Perry. This is suggested by the fact that Pluss goes beyond listening to his patients' stories, gets caught up by them, and eventually seems to go a little mad himself when he quits the sanitarium and disappears. I say "seems" because, mirroring Pluss's dissolution, the narrative strands of the book, which had been tightly wound in the first section that focused closely on Pluss, begin to unravel, with Jonah taking over much of the narrative and becoming a new focal point. This shift of gears can be a bit disorienting as the realism of the opening is partially abandoned, but it does give the reader a chance to see the schizophrenia developing as it gains hold of Pluss's thought processes. Pluss is like the psychiatrist Dr. Dysart in Peter Shaffer's play *Equus*, who begins to doubt his profession, since when a cure succeeded it often converted a passionate, inspired, if addled person into a normal but dull zombie. Pluss is attracted by the crazed creativity of so many of his charges. Unlike Dysart, though, who confines his admiration to rueful ruminations, Pluss mimics his patients, becoming psychotic in the process.

I mentioned previously that Couteau obtained psychological knowledge not only from studying and from thinking about books on the mind but also by reading literature. Indeed, it is important to note that while Pluss took the ultimately dangerous path of learning from his patients, Couteau has deepened his insights by interviewing great writers, such as Ray Bradbury and Hubert Selby Jr.

These interviews are not simple Q&A's but are interactions with a lot of give and take. The interview with Selby (done for *Rain Taxi*) delves deeply into spirituality and ethics. In a notable passage, Selby remarks, "What we seem to be taught, at least in the Western world, is that we're born with a blank slate, and we have to learn how to get and get…. But no one ever seems to train us in methods of finding out that we already have within us all the things that are valuable: all the treasures. But it's only in the process of giving them away, to somebody else, that we become aware of having them."

This thought seems to follow up on insights brought to bear in *Doctor Pluss*. One reason for the immobilization of so many in psychiatric offices or institutions (according to Couteau and the Shaffer of *Equus*) is that conventional education does not provide tools for people to deal with stress or act in a humanitarian, giving manner, only instructing them on how to get ahead.

I can't help, though, but note that Selby, like Couteau, suggests he has learned from unique individuals, pointing to none other than *Evergreen Review's* own editor, Barney Rosset, for special commendation. In discussing his first novel, *Last Exit to Brooklyn*, which Rosset published, Selby engages in an interchange, beginning with Couteau's question: "Why was *Last Exit* allowed to be published in the United States in 1964, while *Tropic of Cancer*, which was a much less obscene book – by the classical definition – was banned until just a few years before this?"

> **Selby**: I think because … it [*Tropic*] had been banned for many years. You could only smuggle it in and all that sort of stuff. So, it had a different resistance and a different procedure to go through.

Couteau: It had an already established weight, a history that it had to deal with.

Selby: Right. Yeah. And of course, Barney Rosset took care of business and made it possible for a lot of things to happen.

It's nice to see that old debts – Rosset's discovery and championing of Selby's work – are here being repaid, but this also brings me to a final thought on history. Some readers may find Couteau out of date, in that Laing and the antipsychiatry movement to which he belonged are not the household names they were in the 1960s, but they (as represented by Perry) seem to orient and spur the author's fictional and nonfictional excursions. While some may say this current of psychology has been superseded, Couteau has a gone a long way toward showing that it still possesses validity and staying power. How else account for the intellectual freshness, richness, and potency of his novel and essays?
– Jim Feast is the author of *Neo-Phobe* and the former assistant editor of the *Evergreen Review*.

THE SLEEPING MERMAID

Novelist and literary enthusiast Rob Couteau brings readers part of his love with *The Sleeping Mermaid*, a book of flowing poetry and thought that asks plenty of questions and offers plenty of answers. *The Sleeping Mermaid* is a poetry collection well-worth considering.
– Willis M. Buhle, *Midwest Book Review*.

In Couteau's work there is no phoniness, no artifice for the sake of artifice – though in the great French tradition this poet knows so well, there is some art for the sake of art. Couteau does not venture into realms of obscurity where meaning is confined to the interior of a Klein bottle; his poems all have direct force, subjects, even verbs. He is intent on having his readers share in his observations, whether it be his artful retelling and reinterpretations of Native American story and song, or his appraisal of how a woman parades across the avenue. He does not ever sacrifice ordinary sense for an extra-ordinary significance. Instead, he speaks with fervor, with something to say, with something he wants us to hang onto and, in the process, come to an understanding of why it matters not just to him but should matter to us. In other words: he knows what he wants to say, and says it.

Couteau's poetic material is as vast as his learning and imagination. And yet he does not seem overly concerned with making tidy themes, or buttoning his knowledge into a small sphere. Indeed, I often sense that he hasn't really selected his material; rather his material seems to have selected him. But obedient to the muse and his own gifts, he records for us with clear-eyed insight the spectrum of his collisions between subject and object, the real and imagined, the read and reread and then reinvented, himself and the perceived, the distillate of being always awake and attentive to what confronts him. Indeed. Couteau is not conditional in his probing of the human condition, even to the point of exposing his own condition in face of what he is examining. He steps right in, and in turn allows us the gift of his informed vision. What we see is not always pretty, nor dressed up for the photo-op. But he never panders. He sees what he sees and puts it down on the page with grace and often beauty. And we, as readers, benefit

enormously for his willingness to go the distance with what
matters.

I think it was William Carlos Williams who said that
poetry is belief. Couteau believes in belief, believes that
poetic worth is measured in faithfulness to what is, what
has been, and what could be. These are his talismans; these
are the points where he begins and ends. His poetic
excursions take us to many places: to the Paris of Rimbaud
and Picasso, to the Native North Americans, to mythology
and history and how the woman he is encountering is
seducing him as he seduces her (and us), and finally, how
alone, the cosmos plays itself out at 3 a.m. when the only
lapdog is memory.

**– A former creative-writing teacher at MIT,
Christopher Sawyer-Lauçanno is the author of *The
Continual Pilgrimage: American Writers in Paris, 1944–
1960* and *An Invisible Spectator, A Biography of Paul
Bowles*.**

www.ingramcontent.com/pod-product-compliance
Lightning Source LLC
Chambersburg PA
CBHW022016120726
47902CB00012B/381